PERSPECTIVES ON EARLY CHILDHOOD PSYCHOLOGY AND EDUCATION

Volume 4, Issue 1
Spring 2019

Copyright © 2019
Pace University Press
41 Park Row
15th floor
New York, NY 10038

ISBN: 978-1-935625-35-3
ISSN: 2471-1527

Member

Council of Editors of Learned Journals

PERSPECTIVES on EARLY CHILDHOOD PSYCHOLOGY and EDUCATION

EDITOR
David E. McIntosh, *Ball State University*

ASSOCIATE EDITORS
Tammy Hughes, *Duquesne University*
Barbara A. Mowder, *Pace University*
Flo Rubinson, *Brooklyn College*

EDITORIAL REVIEW BOARD
Vincent C. Alfonso, *Gonzaga University*
Stephen Bagnato, *University of Pittsburgh*
Renee Bergeron, *Consultant*
Zeynep Biringen, *Colorado State University*
Bruce Bracken, *College of William & Mary*
Melissa Bray, *University of Connecticut*
Victoria Comerchero, *Touro College*
Gerard Costa, *Montclair State University*
Grace Elizade-Utnick, *City University of New York at Brooklyn College*
Nancy Evangelista, *Alfred University*
Kathryn Fletcher, *Ball State University*
Randy Floyd, *University of Memphis*
Gilbert Foley, *New York Center for Child Development*
Laurie Ford, *University of British Columbia*
Pamela Guess, *University of Tennessee*
Robin Hojnoski, *Lehigh University*
Paul McCabe, *Brooklyn College*
Sara McCane-Bowling, *University of Tennessee*
Geraldine Oades-Sese, *Rutgers Robert Wood Johnson Medical School*
Matt Reynolds, *University of Kansas*
Gail Ross, *NY Presbyterian Hospital*
Susan Ruby, *Eastern Washington University*
Mark Sossin, *Pace University*
Esther Stavrou, *Yeshiva University*
Mark Terjesen, *St. John's University*
Lea Theodore, *College of William and Mary*
Mary Ward, *Weill Cornell Medical College*
Adriana Wissel, *Gonzaga University*

TABLE OF CONTENTS

Editor's Note 1
David E. McIntosh

GENERAL ARTICLES

Behavior Rating Scales and the Assessment of Attention
Deficit Hyperactivity Disorder in Early Childhood:
A Review of Psychometric Properties and Scale Features 5
Mark Terjesen, Mark J. Sciutto, and Christine O'Brien

Children's Adjustment to Kindergarten:
Predictions from Mother-Child Emotional Availability
and Children's Narratives Prior to School Entry 39
*Jun Wang, Hannah Wurster, Shauna Skillern Fisher,
Kate Shepard, Jennifer Gerber Moné, and Zeynep Biringen*

Concurrent and Predictive Relationships Between the
Bayley-III and Stanford-Binet 5 71
Laura E. Murphy, Colby D. Taylor, and Randy G. Floyd

Psychometric Properties of a Kindergarten Readiness
Assessment Using Exploratory Structural
Equation Modeling 105
Annie C. Liner, Kathryn L. Fletcher, and Patricia C. Clark

Adult Perceptions of an Inclusive Playground Designed
and Built Based on the Results of Prior Studies Examining
"Dream" Playgrounds 129
Tina L. Stanton-Chapman and Eric L. Schmidt

LIST OF CONTRIBUTORS 149

EDITORIAL POLICY 153

CALL FOR PAPERS 155

Editor's Note

It is a privilege to serve as the second editor for *Perspectives on Early Childhood Psychology and Education*. As the journal enters its fourth year of existence, it is important to revisit the vision of the first editor, Vincent C. Alfonso, who had the foresight to establish a journal focused on publishing original research "relevant to infants, young children (to age 8), families, and caregivers."

Over the next three years, the journal will continue the mission of publishing, high quality, original research. Establishing the journal as an outlet for upcoming and experienced researchers in the fields of psychology and education to publish and disseminate their research relevant to young children will be a primary objective.

Utilizing the journal as an important forum to allow prominent researchers, willing to serve as guest editors, to publish research and transformative theoretical paradigms on emerging topics will also be a primary focus of the journal.

Finally, the journal will continue to serve a valuable role in promoting and accumulating evidenced-based research related to psychological and educational interventions used with young children.

This volume presents a broad range of scholarship reflecting the founding principles and the future directions of *Perspectives on Early Childhood Psychology and Education*.

David E. McIntosh, Editor

GENERAL ARTICLES

Behavior Rating Scales and the Assessment of Attention Deficit Hyperactivity Disorder in Early Childhood: A Review of Psychometric Properties and Scale Features

Mark Terjesen, Mark J. Sciutto, and Christine O'Brien

Abstract

Accurate diagnosis of Attention Deficit Hyperactivity Disorder (ADHD) is complicated by the fact that many young children exhibit the symptoms that are associated with the disorder. The use of behavior rating scales has become an important component of the assessment of ADHD and while there are a number of well-constructed and standardized measures to aid assessment, much of the research focuses on the assessment of children above the age of 5 years. In this study, ADHD behavior rating scales with preschoolers were contrasted based on their psychometric characteristics (e.g., quality of standardization, reliability, validity) and quality of guidelines for interpretation. Although most test manuals reviewed in this study provided sufficient evidence of reliability and validity for ages 5 years and up, most provided less detail about psychometric data with preschoolers. For behavior rating scales to be helpful for assessment of preschoolers, more detailed information of the psychometric properties of these scales with this population is necessary.

***Keywords*: ADHD, preschool, assessment, psychometrics**

Attention Deficit Hyperactive Disorder (ADHD) is a neurodevelopmental disorder characterized by a persistent pattern of inattention and/or hyperactivity-impulsivity and a reduced capacity for behavioral inhibition that interferes with daily functioning (American Psychiatric Association [APA], 2013). According to the 2011–2013 National Health Interview Survey, prevalence of clinically diagnosed ADHD among children 4–5 years of age was 2.7% (Pastor, Reuben, Duran, & Hawkins, 2015). Additional data suggest that in 2011 to 2012, 1.5% of children ages 2–5 had an ADHD diagnosis, compared to 1% in 2007 to 2008 (Danielson et al., 2017). Furthermore, while the number of children receiving treatment for ADHD has risen from 2007 to 2011, up to 17.5% of children with a diagnosis of ADHD were not receiving treatment (Visser et al., 2014). The Centers for Disease Control and Prevention (CDC) recommend behavior therapy as the first line of treatment for ADHD among preschoolers (American Academy of Pediatrics, 2011), but only 53.2% of preschoolers receive the recommended treatment of behavior therapy (Visser et al., 2015). As such, there is a clear gap between diagnosis of ADHD and receipt of services. Perhaps a better understanding as to how ADHD presents itself during the preschool years and how to assess reliably for it would lead to better treatment planning.

ADHD is typically diagnosed during school years; however, there is an increasing tendency for the disorder to be identified in preschoolers (Egger, Kondo, & Angold, 2006; Posner et al., 2007; Thomas, Sanders, Doust, Beller, & Glasziou, 2015). Some researchers have suggested that an earlier onset of symptoms is associated with a greater likelihood of comorbid conditions and subsequent functional impairment (Riddle et al., 2013). Children who were diagnosed with ADHD at ages 4–6 were at a greatly increased risk to meet clinical criteria for depression or for attempting suicide through age 18, as compared to other children (Chronis-Tuscano et al., 2010). Thus, accurately identifying young children with ADHD has clinical utility in terms of preventive mental health work. Further, additional research has supported the link between early childhood behavior problems and later problem behaviors (Diamantopoulou, Rydell, Thorell, & Bohlin, 2007; Wåhlstedt, Thorell, & Bohlin 2008; Weyandt, 2007) and academic functioning (Breslau et al., 2009; Diamantopoulou et al., 2007). In a two-year study of preschool children ages 2–4, Wåhlstedt, Thornell and Bohlin (2008) found ADHD symptoms predicted later problems in socioemotional functioning. Further, high levels of ADHD symptoms were associated with a broad spectrum of social functioning issues including emotion regulation and social competence (Wåhlstedt et al., 2008). Children with ADHD are also significantly more likely to develop a conduct disorder in adolescence and antisocial personality disorder in adulthood, thus increasing their risk for substance use disorders and subsequent incarceration, than their peers without ADHD (APA, 2013).

Preschool children with ADHD commonly suffer comorbid conditions, such as oppositional defiant disorder (ODD), anxiety disorders, and communication disorders (Bendiksen et al., 2014; Posner et al., 2007), and these children tend to have lower overall functioning than those with ADHD alone (Egger et al., 2006). Accurate diagnosis and subsequent treatment are important, given that individuals with ADHD who do not receive treatment have poorer long-term outcomes compared to those who receive treatment (Shaw et al., 2012). Accordingly, early identification of ADHD symptoms may allow for the development of intervention strategies to maximize the child's potential and prevent future difficulties. However, accurate assessment and diagnosis of ADHD in early childhood is often difficult (Smith & Corkum, 2007; Steinhoff et al., 2006). Because the hallmark symptoms of ADHD occur to some extent in most children and may be the result of other conditions, the identification of clinically disordered inattention and hyperactivity can be more problematic (Mahone, 2005). Accurate assessment of ADHD often requires information about the extent to which these behaviors deviate from age-appropriate levels (Anastopoulos & Shelton, 2001; Campbell, Halperin, & Sonuga-Barke, 2014). For example, it is more difficult at these ages to distinguish between normal and abnormal levels of hyperactivity, impulsivity and inattention (Healey, Miller, Castelli, Marks, & Haleprin, 2008; Terjesen & Kurasaki, 2009). Globally, inattention and hyperactivity are common developmental features among preschool children (Smith, 2011). That is, the symptoms of ADHD are ubiquitous and age-relevant, presenting unique challenges of assessing ADHD in very young children (Smith, 2011). Although it can be challenging to distinguish between typical development and clinical symptomatology, Smith (2011) hypothesizes that ADHD can be reliably diagnosed in children as young as 3 years, through the use of thorough evaluations.

As a result, behavior rating scales have become an indispensable part of the assessment of ADHD because they provide normative information about the extent of the child's symptoms in multiple settings, such as in school and at home (Merrell, 2007). Shapiro and Heick (2004) found that, among school psychologists, behavior rating scales are among the most frequently used assessment tools and that their use has increased substantially over the past decade. Behavior rating scales also have clinical utility in terms of progress monitoring of the effectiveness of an intervention within the schools (Chezan, Kratochwill, Terjesen, & Nguyen, 2017). Rating scales are fundamental in the assessment of ADHD, mainly because information from various informants (i.e., parents and teachers) is provided (Tobin, Schneider, & Landau, 2014). Discrepancies among different informants' ratings of child psychopathology are common (De Los Reyes & Kazdin, 2005). In addition to data from multiple informants, best practices in the assessment of ADHD include the utilization of multiple methods, including diagnostic interviews and systematic direct observation in naturalistic settings (Tobin et al., 2014). However, there are no established guidelines for integrating assessment data across sources and methods, or for resolving informant discrepancies (Tobin et al., 2014).

There are numerous well-constructed and nationally standardized behavior rating scales to aid clinicians in their assessment of ADHD. In a survey of school psychologists' use of specific measures for ADHD, Demaray, Scahefer, and DeLong (2003) found that most frequently reported scales were the Connors instruments, the Behavior Assessment System for Children (BASC), the Attention Deficit Disorder Evaluation Scale (ADDES), the Home Situation Questionnaire, the School Situation Questionnaire and the Child Behavior Check List (CBCL). Magnusson et al. (2006) found that self-report scales and informant scales predicted interview-based diagnoses in childhood and adulthood with adequate sensitivities and specificities. There have also been several thorough reviews of the psychometric characteristics of these scales for the assessment of ADHD (e.g., Anastopoulos & Shelton, 2001; Connor, 2002; Demaray, Elting, & Schaefer, 2003; McGough & McCracken, 2000; Pelham, Fabiano, & Massetti, 2005; Smith & Corkum, 2007). However, with one exception, much of this literature focuses on the assessment of children above the age of 5 years. Smith and Corkum (2007) focused on very young children: they analyzed data from peer-reviewed studies on the quality of various tools (e.g., rating scales, interviews, observational measures) used in the assessment or diagnosis of ADHD in preschoolers.

In addition to reviewing the psychometric properties, they also examined the symptom descriptions and logistics for each of the measures, assigning them quality indicators. While the text highlights some of the psychometrics of the rating scales, specifics as to what constituted ratings of "satisfied minimal criteria" were not apparent. In addition, the authors reviewed four behavior rating scales and also included psychometrics from additional research sources that may not be available to the practitioner for making decisions about which test to use. The authors concluded that there is a need for more developmentally appropriate measures of ADHD in preschoolers. Unfortunately, limited information is available to help clinicians select the most appropriate behavior rating scale for children under the age of 6 years. In 2011, the American Academy of Pediatrics published new clinical recommendations for the diagnosis and evaluation of ADHD in children, in which they expanded the age ranges to include preschool children as young as 4 years of age

(American Academy of Pediatrics, 2011). Given these new guidelines, behavior rating scales must be evaluated to ensure appropriateness for use with preschool children.

In sum, behavior rating scales have typically shown good psychometric properties with school-age children (age 6 years and up). However, relatively little is known about the properties of these measures with younger children (i.e., ages 2–5) with the last review published in 2007 (Smith & Corkum, 2007). Since that review, there have been considerable updates to existing measures of ADHD that warrant review to assist clinicians and researchers in determining which rating scale to use, as each scale has unique features that may make it more appropriate for specific uses. By reviewing updated versions of measures for preschoolers, specifying criteria as to what is considered to constitute "acceptable" psychometrics as well as including only data for review that is publically available to the researcher and practitioner, this study will add to the Smith and Corkum review.

In this study, we examine the psychometric and technical characteristics of various published measures of ADHD that can be used with preschool age children. In addition, we will highlight important distinguishing features among the various behavior rating scales so that clinicians can more effectively select measures that will be most useful for assessment of ADHD in preschool children.

Method

Scale Identification

An extensive literature search was conducted to find what ADHD scales are publicly available (either published in a peer-reviewed journal or available to purchase) to screen and measure for the presence of ADHD symptoms among preschool age children. A search was conducted using electronic databases, including PsycARTICLES (EBSCO & APA), PsycInfo, ERIC, and Proquest Psychology sites using the keywords: ADHD, ADD, preschool, early childhood, children, assessment, and evaluation. Additionally, an electronic search of the Buros Institute of Mental Measurements was conducted. As this was a study of published measures, a search of the online catalogs of psychological tests published by testing companies also took place: Multi-Health Systems Inc., Psychological Assessment Resources Inc., PsychCorp, Riverside, and Western Psychological Services.

Rating Scales

Table 1 presents a list of the behavior rating scales evaluated in this study. Assessments were included in this review if they were (a) commercially available; (b) contained normative data for children under the age of 6 years; and (c) described as an ADHD assessment. Because the utility of a particular rating scale depends on the purpose of the assessment (Sattler, 2014; DuPaul & Stoner, 2014), broadband and narrowband instruments were included.

Table 1
Behavior Rating Scales

Scale type	Scale name
Broadband	Behavior Assessment System for Children: Third Edition (BASC-3; Reynolds & Kamphaus, 2015)
	Child Behavior Checklist (CBCL/1½–5; Achenbach & Rescorla, 2000) Caregiver-Teacher Report Form (C-TRF/1½–5; Achenbach & Rescorla, 2000)
	Conners Early Childhood (Conners, 2009)
Narrowband	ADHD Rating Scale-V (DuPaul, Power, Anastopoulos, & Reid, 2016)
	Brown Attention Deficit Disorder Scales (Brown, 2001)
	Early Childhood Attention Deficit Disorders Evaluation Scale (ECADDES; McCarney, 1995)
	ADHD Comprehensive Teacher Rating Scale (ACTeRS; Ullmann, Sleator, & Sprague, 2000)

Evaluation Criteria

In general, each of the scales in Table 1 is supported by extensive research and has demonstrated very good psychometric properties. However, previous reviews have typically focused on the use of these scales for the assessment of children over the age of 5 years. The purpose of this study is to evaluate the properties and features of these scales for use with preschool children. For each of the measurements presented in Table 1, we evaluated and reviewed the accompanying manual for information on the following criteria:

Norms and standardization. Using guidelines presented by Hammill, Brown, and Bryant (1994), we analyzed the standardization sample of each measure by reviewing the size of the normative group, the match of demographic characteristics of the normative group to the United States population, and the recency of normative data. In addition, we noted the availability of alternative norms (e.g., gender, clinical, ethnicity) that a clinician could use to supplement comparisons to general population norms.

Scale features. In addition to the psychometric characteristics of behavior ratings scales, psychologists must also consider the specific purpose for which an assessment tool is to be used. In the case of behavior rating scales, each scale typically has several unique features that may make it more or less desirable for a specific purpose. Specifically, we noted the presence or absence of several features that may influence a clinician's decision to use a particular measure. These features were:

1. **Scale length.** We noted the number of items for the entire scale as well as for the ADHD specific components (if different from the total scale). Longer scales typically provide more detailed information about specific problem behaviors and tend to be more reliable, but require more time to administer and score. Depending on the specific purpose of the assessment (e.g., screening), scale length may be an important factor.

2. **Diagnostic Statistical Manual (DSM) criteria**. We coded whether the items were derived from or closely linked to the DSM-IV (APA, 1994) or DSM-5 (APA, 2013) criteria for the diagnosis of ADHD. Scale items that closely mirror the DSM criteria may reduce some of the subjectivity inherent in the implementation of those criteria.
3. **Inattention and hyperactivity/impulsivity subscales.** Factor analytic studies of the symptoms of ADHD have typically yielded two primary clusters of symptoms: inattention and hyperactive/impulsive (Burns, Boe, Walsh, Sommers-Flanagan, & Teegarden, 2001; Manning & Miller, 2001; Ryser, Campbell, & Miller, 2010). The current Diagnostic and Statistical Manual of Mental Disorders criteria maintains the distinction between these two clusters. The DSM-5 criteria are similar to the DSM-IV criteria. The most important changes involve the inclusion of a severity specifier, the changing of the age of onset from before 7 years of age to before 12 years, the lowering of symptom requirement from 6 to 5 symptoms for ages 17 or older, and new categories for individuals who do not meet the full criteria. Accordingly, we recorded whether each scale allows for differentiation of the two primary clusters of ADHD symptoms as specified in the DSM-5. Separate subscales for the two symptom clusters may be particularly useful for determining the ADHD presentation.

Validity scales. Behavior ratings scales are not equivalent to direct observation measures. Accordingly, they are measures of opinion or perception, and "are subject to the same oversights, prejudices, and limitations on reliability and validity such opinions may have" (Barkley, 1997, p. 97). Behavior rating scales yield information that may be influenced by (a) halo effects; (b) general attitudes toward the child; (c) the rater's internal states; and (d) the rater's tolerance for misbehavior (Hinshaw & Nigg, 1999; Mandal, Olmi, & Wilczynski, 1999; Reid & Maag, 1994). The potential for rater bias may be particularly important when the parents or teachers have a stake in the results of the assessment (e.g., custody evaluations, educational placement, eligibility for services). In this study, we assessed whether the scale allows the clinician to assess the extent to which respondents are attempting to minimize or exaggerate the severity of the child's symptoms.

Reliability. Reliability refers to the extent to which test scores are free from errors of measurement (American Educational Research Association [AERA], APA, & National Council on Measurement in Education [NCME], 2014). Consistent with the recommendations of Hammill et al. (1994), the following estimates of reliability were evaluated: internal consistency, test-retest reliability, and interrater reliability. Anastasi (1982) recommends a reliability coefficient of .80 or above as indicative of good reliability for a brief scale.

Validity. Validity refers to how well a test measures the characteristics or dimensions it purports to measure. AERA, APA, and NCME (2014) recommend ideal validation would be demonstrated in three dimensions: construct validity, criterion-related validity, and content validity. Construct validity is the extent to which a measure is measuring precisely the construct that it intends to measure and no similar measures. Establishing construct validity is a process of gathering evidence of convergent and discriminant validity (AERA, APA, & NCME, 2014). Criterion-related validity can be described as when test scores are related to performance on a particular criterion (AERA, APA, & NCME, 2014). AERA, APA, and NCME describe content validity as evidence that the items on the instrument measure the domain it is intended to represent. Some have argued that some forms of validity (i.e., content, criterion) are most appropriately subsumed under construct validity and can be viewed as evidence for the construct validity rather than distinct types of validity (Messick, 1995). Unfortunately, this view is not universally recognized in practice and the many forms of validity are not used consistently (Kazdin, 2002).

Because most of the manuals used in this study specify evidence for the different types of validity, for the purposes of this study, we make distinctions among the information presented on each type of validity.

In addition to these psychometric properties, it is also essential to understand how useful a measure is for making important clinical decisions. Most behavior rating scales employ a cutoff score that indicates a clinically significant deviation from age-appropriate levels of behavior. The clinical utility of a measure derives from the extent to which cutoff scores result in correct identification or misidentification of ADHD children. Clinical utility is a function of the measure's positive predictive power (PPP), negative predictive power (NPP), sensitivity, and specificity (Power & Ikeda, 1996; Reid & Maag, 1994).[1] PPP and sensitivity are useful for "ruling in" a specific disorder. NPP and specificity are useful for "ruling out" a specific disorder.

Results and Discussion

Norms and Standardization

The age ranges covered by scales varied with few providing norms across the entire 2–5 year range (see Table 2). In general, standardization procedures were clearly described in the manuals. Details about scale construction, item analysis, and sample selection were both accessible and well organized. Standardization samples were generally of sufficient size and the authors reported that they attempted to be representative of the United States population (see Table 3). However, there were some exceptions. Minority children and children from the western regions of the United States were underrepresented in the standardization sample for the Early Childhood

---

1. Positive predictive power refers to the probability that a child would be given a particular diagnosis (ADHD in this case) given that he or she scores above a certain level on a given scale (e.g., Conners ADHD Index). Negative predictive power refers to the probability that a child would not be given an ADHD diagnosis when he or she scores below a given cutoff score. Sensitivity is the probability that children from a known index group (e.g., ADHD children) score at or above a particular cutoff point. Specificity is the probability that children who do not have ADHD will score below a particular cutoff point.

Table 2
Ages Covered by Norms of ADHD Rating Scales

	Age (years)			
Scale	2	3	4	5
ACTeRS—Teacher form				●[a]
ACTeRS—Parent form				●
ADHD-V—Home				●
ADHD-V—School				●
BASC-3—Parent	●	●	●	●
BASC-3—Teacher	●	●	●	●
Brown ADD—Parent		●[b]	●	●
Brown ADD—Teacher		●[b]	●	●
CBCL—Parent	●	●	●	●
C-TRF	●	●	●	●
Conners Early Childhood—Parent	●	●	●	●
Conners Early Childhood—Teacher	●	●	●	●
ECADDES—Home	●	●	●	●
ECADDES—School	●	●	●	●

Note. ACTeRS = ADHD Comprehensive Teacher Rating Scale; ADHD-V = ADHD Rating Scale-V; BASC-3 = Behavior Assessment System for Children: Third Edition; Brown ADD = Brown Attention-Deficit Disorder Scales; CBCL = Achenbach Child Behavior Checklist; C-TRF = Achenbach Caregiver-Teacher Report Form; ECADDES = Early Childhood Attention Deficit Disorders Evaluation Scale.
[a] Available for grades K-8, but not specifically differentiated by age.
[b] Available for ages 3-12.

Attention Disorders Evaluation Scale (ECADDES). Likewise, the caregiver/teacher rating form of the CBCL (i.e., ages 2–5) lacked sufficient geographic diversity among the standardization sample. Furthermore, the ADD Comprehensive Teacher's Rating Scale (ACTeRS) manual made no mention of considering ethnicity or geographic region in their norm sample.

Significant differences in the severity of ADHD symptoms across gender (Thorell & Rydell, 2008; Merikangas et al., 2010) and ethnicity (Pastor & Reuben, 2005; Pastor et al., 2015) have been well docu-

Table 3
Characteristics of Standardization Samples for ADHD Rating Scales

	Normative sample size			
Scale	Total	Under 6	Year	Represent U.S. population
ACTeRS—Teacher form	2,362	150[a]	1989[b]	NP
ACTeRS—Parent form	892	NP	NP	NP
ADHD-V—Home (ages 5–7)	2079	475	2015	Y
ADHD-V—School (ages 5–7)	2140	465	2015	Y
BASC-3—Parent	1800	600	2015	Y
BASC-3—Teacher	1700	500	2015	Y
Brown ADD—Parent	800	199	2001	Y
Brown ADD—Teacher	800	195	2001	Y
CBCL (ages 1½–5)	700	700	2000	Y[c]
C-TRF (ages 1½–5)	1192	1192	2000	Y[c]
Conners Early Childhood—Parent Short form Long form	800 800	640 640	2009 2009	Y Y
Conners Early Childhood—Teacher Short form Long form	800 800	640 640	2009 2009	Y Y
ECADDES—Home (ages 2–5)	2009	1720	1995	N[c]
ECADDES—School (ages 2–5)	2887	2776	1995	N[c]

Note. NP = Information Not Provided; ACTeRS = ADHD Comprehensive Teacher Rating Scale; ADHD-V = ADHD Rating Scale-IV; BASC-3 = Behavior Assessment System for Children: Third Edition; Brown ADD = Brown Attention-Deficit Disorder Scales; CBCL = Achenbach Child Behavior Checklist; C-TRF = Achenbach Caregiver-Teacher Report Form; ECADDES = Early Childhood Attention Deficit Disorders Evaluation Scale.
[a] Authors report approximately 150 students in each of the lower grades (K-5) were included to provide a check on the stability of the norms.
[b] Authors report that in 1989 a large-scale study to expand the norms was initiated. Latest version of manual was published in 2000. [c] U.S. census data were not specifically used, but an effort was made to obtain a sample that was representative of the population.

mented. However, general population norms typically provided by behavior rating scales may pool these disparate groups together. Consequently, when using general norms to evaluate developmental deviance, some groups (e.g., males, African Americans) may be over-identified as ADHD because the "cutoff score" is lowered by the presence of other groups (e.g., females, Caucasians) in the normative sample (Reid et al., 2000). To address this concern, some researchers have advocated the use of subgroup norms that provide normative comparisons within the context of group membership (Hinshaw & Nigg, 1999; Reid et al., 2000). In this study, we recorded whether the scale offers additional norms (e.g., gender, ethnicity, clinical) that the clinician can use as an alternative or as a supplement to general norms (see Table 4).

All of the scales provided separate gender norms but only the Behavioral Assessment System of Children, third edition (BASC-3) provided clinical norms. None of the scales reviewed provided separate norms based on ethnicity. The lack of race or ethnicity norms, however, is likely due to the relatively small number of racial or ethnic minorities in the standardization sample. For example, to obtain a sufficient number of African American children at each age group and maintain a representative sample of the United States population, standardization samples would need to be substantially larger. Ethnicity was only discussed from the extent to which ethnic minorities were represented in the standardization sample. Similar to the clinical norms, several scales (i.e., BASC-3, Conners EC Short and Long Forms) provided means and *SD*s for different ethnic groups but not standard score conversions. The availability of alternative norms may provide the clinician with valuable information that is not available via general norms. Alternative norms may allow a clinician to address concerns over ceiling effects and the over- or under-identification of certain children.

One consistent concern among the scales, however, was the tendency to pool normative data across the entire preschool age range. In some cases (i.e., the ACTeRS and the Brown ADD), normative information about preschool age children was combined with information about older children (e.g., 4–11 year olds). In these cases, it was more difficult to evaluate the quality of the standardization samples for preschool children specifically. Pooling across age groups

Table 4
Available Norms for Preschool Age Population

Scale	Ethnicity	Gender	Clinical
ACTeRS—Teacher form		•	
ACTeRS—Parent form		•	
ADHD-V—Home (ages 5–7)		•	•[a]
ADHD-V—School (ages 5–7)		•	•[a]
BASC-3—Parent (ages 2–18)	•[a]	•	•
BASC-3—Teacher (ages 2–18)	•[a]	•	•
Brown ADD Scales—Parent (ages 3–5)		•	
Brown ADD Scales—Teacher (ages 3–5)		•	
CBCL—Parent (ages 1½–5)		•	
C-TRF (ages 1½–5)		•	
Conners Early Childhood—Parent rating scales			
Short form	•[a]	•	
Long form	•[a]	•	•
Conners Early Childhood—Teacher rating scales			
Short form	•[a]	•	
Long form	•[a]	•	•[a]
ECADDES—Home		•	
ECADDES—School		•	

Note. ACTeRS = ADHD Comprehensive Teacher Rating Scale; ADHD-V = ADHD Rating Scale-V; BASC-3 = Behavior Assessment System for Children: Third Edition; Brown ADD = Brown Attention-Deficit Disorder Scales; CBCL = Achenbach Child Behavior Checklist; C-TRF = Achenbach Caregiver-Teacher Report Form; ECADDES = Early Childhood Attention Deficit Disorders Evaluation Scale.
[a] Manual provides means and standard deviations, but does not provide standard score conversions.

assumes that the psychometric properties of the scale are consistent across development.

Scale Features

The varied features of the ADHD rating scales are presented in Table 5. Only the BASC-3 and Conners EC short forms included a validity scale (e.g., fake bad) and only the Conners EC included a mechanism (i.e., positive impression) for evaluating respondents' tendency to minimize a child's symptoms (i.e., fake good). In most cases, the manuals neglected consideration of response bias altogether. Depending on the purpose of the assessment (e.g., eligibility for services), information about response bias could be extremely important. With very young children who may not be in any type of school on a regular basis, a validity scale may be especially important because the parent is the only source of information on the child (De Los Reyes et al., 2015; Shelton & Barkley, 1993). Scales varied considerably in length and specificity. The BASC-3, the Conners EC long form, and the Child Behavior Checklists are broadband rating scales that evaluate characteristics other than ADHD symptoms, but take longer to complete. The ADHD-V, Brown Attention Deficit Disorder Scales, ACTeRS, and the ECADDES may be preferable when information about ADHD-related symptoms only is needed. The Conners EC short form has 49 (parent) and 48 (teacher/childcare) items that were chosen from data collected on the full-length norms and has six items that measure inattention/hyperactivity.

Separate inattention and hyperactivity/impulsivity scales may be important for making accurate diagnosis of ADHD symptom presentations. All rating scales except the Conners EC and the CBCL made this distinction, although not all linked this distinction to either the DSM-IV or DSM-5 criteria. The CBCL provides an attention problems scale but not a pure hyperactivity/impulsivity scale. Instead, the CBCL provides a total externalizing problems scale, which includes aspects of hyperactivity and impulsivity, but also includes aggression, delinquency, and oppositional behaviors. An interesting feature of

Table 5
ADHD Rating Scale Features

Scale	Total items	ADHD items	Derived from DSM?	Symptom cluster subscales?	Validity scale(s)
ACTeRS—Teacher form	24	24	N	Y[a]	N
ACTeRS—Parent form	25	25	N	Y[a]	N
ADHD-V—Home	18	18	Y	Y	N
ADHD-V—School	18	18	Y	Y	N
BASC-3—Parent (ages 2–5)	139	18	Y	Y[b]	Y[c]
BASC-3—Teacher (ages 2–5)	105	16	Y	Y[b]	Y[c]
Brown ADD Scales—Parent (ages 3–5)	44	44	Y	Y[d]	N
Brown ADD Scales—Teacher (ages 3–5)	44	44	Y	Y[d]	N
CBCL (ages 1½–5)	99	5[e]	N	Y	N
C-TRF (ages 1½–5)	99	9[e]	N	Y	N
Conners Early Childhood—Parent					
Short form	49	6	Y	N	Y
Long form	190	16	Y	N	Y
Conners Early Childhood—Teacher					
Short form	48	6	Y	N	Y
Long form	186	20	Y	N	Y
ECADDES—Home	50	50	Y	Y	N
ECADDES—School	56	56	Y	Y	N

Note. ACTeRS = ADHD Comprehensive Teacher Rating Scale; ADHD-V = ADHD Rating Scale-V; BASC-3 = Behavior Assessment System for Children: Third Edition; Brown ADD = Brown Attention-Deficit Disorder Scales; CBCL = Achenbach Child Behavior Checklist; C-TRF = Achenbach Caregiver-Teacher Report Form; Conners = Conners Rating Scales-Revised; ECADDES = Early Childhood Attention Deficit Disorders Evaluation Scale.
[a] Provides factor scales for Attention and Hyperactivity.
[b] Contains an attention problems subscale and an externalizing behavior subscale, but no subscale that specifically measures hyperactivity/impulsivity.
[c] Cutoff point provided to alert clinician to possible symptom "exaggeration or misunderstanding."
[d] Subscales are provided for Inattention Total Score and ADD Combined Total Score.
[e] Items do not constitute a specific scale or subscale.

the CBCL is that the parent and the caregiver-teacher report form provide a profile of DSM-oriented scales, among which is ADHD. These scales align to some extent with DSM diagnostic categories. For the teacher rating, this DSM-oriented scale for ADHD includes 13 items with seven of the items being identical to the attention problems scale, and most of the other items coming from the aggressive behavior subscale. For the parent rating there are six total items on the DSM-oriented ADHD scale with three of them being identical to the attention problem scale. The number of items in the DSM-oriented ADHD scale, especially for the parent rating form, may discourage using the scale solely for diagnostic purposes.

Reliability

Information on the reliability of each of the behavior rating scales is presented in Table 6. All of the scales evaluated in this study, with the exception of the ACTeRS, have demonstrated good to excellent internal consistency for preschool samples. The ACTeRS reports good internal consistency, but does not report it specifically for the preschool level.

Because each of these rating scales measures relatively stable attributes, test-retest stability should be high. Despite considerable variability in test-retest intervals (i.e., 1 week to 8 weeks), the stability coefficients for each of the scales in this study typically exceeded .80. However, test-retest coefficients for preschool age children specifically were not reported in several instances. Only the ECADDES provided test-retest coefficients for each year within the preschool age range.

In general, the inter-rater agreement was good for each of the scales. With the exception of the ADHD-V, Brown ADD Scales, and the ACTeRS, all of the scales reported inter-parent agreement. The ADHD-V scale reported parent-teacher agreement. Inter-rater agreement was typically the lowest of the three forms of reliability, which is neither unexpected nor problematic due to the possibility of true situational differences between home and school or between

Table 6
Reliability of ADHD Rating Scales for Preschoolers

Scale	Internal consistency	Test-Retest (interval in weeks)	Inter-rater agreement		
			T–T	T–P	P–P
ACTeRS—Teacher form					
Attention (grades K–5)	.96	.78 (N)	.61	N	NA
Hyperactivity (grades K–5)	.93	.81 (N)	.73	N	NA
ACTeRS—Parent form					
Attention	.93 [a]	N	NA	N	N
Hyperactivity	.86 [a]	N	NA	N	N
ADHD-V—Home [b]					
Total	N	N (6)	NA	.N	N
Inattention	N	N (6)	NA	N	N
Hyper/imp	N	N (6)	NA	N	N
ADHD-V—School [b]					
Total	N	N (6)	NA	N	NA
Inattention	N	N (6)	NA	N	NA
Hyper/imp	N	N (6)	NA	N	NA
BASC-3—Parent (ages 2–5)					
Attention problems	.86 [a]	.80 (70)	NA	N	.65
Hyperactivity	.86 [a]	.91 (70)	NA	N	.67
BASC-3—Teacher (ages 2–5)					
Attention problems	.90 [a]	.86 (72)	.62	N	NA
Hyperactivity	.90 [a]	.90 (72)	.70	N	NA
Brown ADD Scale—Parent (ages 3–7)					
ADD inattention scale	.96	.78 (1–4)	NA	59	N
ADD combined scale	.97	.78 (1–4)	NA	.60	N
Brown ADD Scale—Teacher (ages 3–7)					
ADD inattention scale	.97	.88 (1–4)	N	.59	NA
ADD combined scale	.98	.89 (14)	N	.60	NA
Child behavior checklist—Parent (ages 1½–5)					
Attention problems	.68	.78 (1)	NA	N	N
Total externalizing	.92	.87 (1)	NA	N	N
Attention deficit/hyperactivity problems	.95	.74 (1)	NA	N	N
Total problems	.78	.90 (1)	NA	N	N
Caregiver-Teacher report form (C-TRF; ages 1½–5)					
Attention problems	.89	.84 (1)	N	N	N
Total externalizing	.96	.89 (1)	N	N	N
Attention deficit/hyperactivity Problems	.97	.79 (1)	N	N	N
Total problems	.92	.88 (1)	N	N	N
Conners Early Childhood—Parent					
Short form	.78	.83	NA	NA	.65
Long form	.86	.87	NA	NA	.72

Table 6 Continued
Reliability of ADHD Rating Scales for Preschoolers

Conners Early Childhood—Teacher					
Short form	.84	90	N	NA	NA
Long form	.89	.93	N	NA	NA
ECADDES—Home					
Total	.98	.86 (4)	NA	NA	.71
Inattentive	.96	.86 (4)	NA	NA	.72
Hyper/imp	.97	.87 (4)	NA	NA	.70
ECADDES—School					
Total	.99	.96 (4)	.67	NA	NA
Inattentive	.98	.95 (4)	.64	NA	NA
Hyper/imp	.99	.97 (4)	.66	NA	NA

Note. ACTeRS = ADHD Comprehensive Teacher Rating Scale; ADHD-V = ADHD Rating Scale-V; BASC-3 = Behavior Assessment System for Children: Third Edition; Brown ADD = Brown Attention-Deficit Disorder Scales; CBCL = Achenbach Child Behavior Checklist; C-TRF = Achenbach Caregiver-Teacher Report Form; ECADDES = Early Childhood Attention Deficit Disorders Evaluation Scale. T–T = inter-rater agreement between two teachers. T–P = inter-rater agreement between a teacher and a parent/caregiver. P–P = inter-rater agreement between two parents/caregivers.
[a] When more than one reliability coefficient was reported in the manual (e.g., for males and females), the mean is presented.
[b] Numbers only presented when available for preschool ages specifically. When this information could have been provided but the manual failed to do so, N was used. When this information was not applicable to the manual, NA was used.

parents. The only scale missing information on inter-rater agreement was the ACTeRS.

In sum, there appears to be solid evidence for the reliability of each of the scales evaluated in this study and this information was relatively easy to decipher from the user manuals. There was some evidence that estimates of reliability differed across age ranges (e.g., 2–3 year olds versus 4–5 year olds). In many cases, these differences were hard to decipher because many manuals do not present reliability information across age groups within the preschool range. Frequently, data for preschool age children were pooled together with older children, which may not be appropriate. For instance, significant age differences in presentation of hyperactive symptoms as children progress through preschool to school age

(Bunte, Schoemaker, Hessen, van der Heijden, & Matthys, 2014; Curchack-Lichtin, Chacko, & Halperin, 2014).

Validity

Evaluation of validity information for a particular scale is a complex process involving the integration of multiple pieces of evidence. Because the validity of a score depends on the purpose for which the scale is being used, it would be inappropriate to make a blanket statement about any one scale's validity, and a more detailed evaluation of the specific support for the various types of validity for each scale is beyond the scope of this study. We refer the reader to published reviews for such information (Demaray et al., 2003; Volpe & DuPaul, 2001). Instead, we focused on the availability of evidence in the manuals for the validity of these scales for the assessment of preschool age children specifically.

In our examination of manuals, there was considerable variability in the way validity information was presented. In some cases, clear distinctions were made between criterion validity and construct validity (or discriminant validity). In other cases, research findings were presented but without clearly distinguishing among the various forms of validity. For our purposes, we focused on the three forms of validity delineated by AERA, APA, and NCME (2014), and the extent to which the manuals provided reasonable evidence of these forms of validity for use with preschool age children specifically. With regard to content validity, all scales contained items that address relevant problem behaviors and appeared to be representative of the entire domain of ADHD problem behaviors. The ADHD-V, Brown ADD Scales, the Conners Rating Scales, and the ECADDES are all specifically linked to the DSM-IV or DSM-5 criteria. The CBCL assesses similar content, but was not specifically derived from or connected to the DSM criteria. In addition, the BASC-3 software provides a link to a number of specific items related to DSM criteria. Furthermore, although authors of the ACTeRS make note of the DSM-IV on the first page of the section describing the design of the scale, they never indicate that they utilized it in item development. The only scale linked to a specific theory of ADHD was the Brown ADD scales, which is linked to executive functioning impairment clusters.

All manuals provided a discussion of convergent and discriminant evidence for construct validity. In some cases, (i.e., with the broadband measures) the evidence was broad and did not refer to the scales specific to ADHD. Additionally, some validity information was only available for certain age ranges. It was often unclear as to whether the scale possessed similar psychometric properties for preschool ages.

All manuals presented adequate evidence of criterion validity. However, it was often difficult to decipher which results were applicable to preschool age children specifically. Only the ADHD-V scale provided information on clinical utility in referencing studies using the earlier version of the scale. This is a significant area of concern. Most scales provide no basis on which to evaluate the extent to which a particular scale's guidelines (i.e., cutoff scores) result in false positives or false negatives. Many of the symptoms of ADHD are common to other childhood disorders, and the ability to make an accurate differential diagnosis depends on using measures that have high PPP and high NPP. Research has suggested that the diagnosis of ADHD may be particularly susceptible to false positives (e.g., Bruchmüller, Margraf, & Schneider, 2012). Unresolved questions exist concerning diagnosis of ADHD. First, some studies suggest a potential overdiagnosis. Second, compared with the male–female ratio in the general population (3:1). Focusing on the conventional psychometric properties alone is likely to present an incomplete picture of the scale's validity).

Overall Quality Indicator of Scales Reviewed

To provide an overall evaluation of the psychometric properties of each scale discussed above, quality point indicators were assigned for each scale based on the categories reviewed. The specific quantification of point values for each of the scales is based on the

Table 7
ADHD Rating Scales for Preschoolers—Quantification of Test Quality

Category	Quality points
Internal consistency reliability	Correlation coefficient ≥.80 = 1 point
Test-retest reliability	Correlation coefficient ≥.80 = 1 point
Interrater reliability	Correlation coefficient ≥.80 = 1 point
Sample size	0 ≤ x < 150 subjects = 0 points 150 ≤ x < 500 subjects = 1 point 500 ≤ x < 1,000 subjects = 2 points 1,000 or more subjects = 3 points
Available norms	Ethnicity = 1 point Gender = 1 point Clinical = 1 point
Validity scales	If present = 1 point
Diversity of sample	Effort made for representative sample = 1 point Matched to U.S. census data = 2 points
Age range assessed	2 years + = 3 points 3 years + = 2 points 4 years + = 1 point 5 years + = 0 points Age ranges beyond 3 years = 0 points
DSM-IV	Coordination with DSM-IV criteria = 1 point
DSM-5	Coordination with DSM-5 criteria = 1 point
Symptom cluster subscales	Factor scales for attention and hyperactivity

work of Klein (2014) and are provided in Table 7. The point values assigned were reviewed by two of the authors and where there was disagreement, it was discussed until consensus was reached. The specific category and overall quality indicators for all scales are reflected in Table 8. Based on this evaluation, the ratings scales that received the highest quality indicators are the BASC-3 and the

Table 8
ADHD Rating Scale and Subscale Quantification of Test Quality for a Preschool Population

Scales	Internal consistency	Test-retest	Inter-rater	Sample size	Available norms	Validity scales	Sample diversity	Age range	DSM	Symptom subscales	Total quality
ACTeRS Teacher	1	0	0	3	1	0	0	0	0	1	6
ACTeRS Parent	1	0	0	2	1	0	0	0	0	1	5
ADHD-V Home (5–7)	0	0	0	3	1	0	2	0	1	1	8
ADHD-V School (5–7)	0	0	0	3	1	0	2	0	1	1	8
BASC-3 Parent (2–5)	1	1	1	3	3	1	2	3	1	1	17
BASC-3 Teacher (2–5)	1	1	1	3	3	1	2	3	1	1	17
Brown ADD Parent (3–5)	1	0	0	2	1	0	2	2	1	1	10
Brown ADD Teacher (3–5)	1	1	0	2	1	0	2	2	1	1	11
CBCL (1½–5)	1	1	0	2	1	0	1	3	0	1	10
C-TRF (1½–5)	1	1	0	3	1	0	1	3	0	1	11

Assessment of ADHD in Early Childhood

Scales	Internal consistency	Test-retest	Inter-rater	Sample size	Available norms	Validity scales	Sample diversity	Age range	DSM	Symptom subscales	Total quality
Conners Parent (Short form)	1	1	0	2	2	1	2	3	1	0	13
Conners Parent (Long form)	1	1	0	2	3	1	2	3	1	0	14
Conners Teacher (Short form)	1	1	0	2	2	1	2	3	1	0	13
Conners Teacher (Long form)	1	1	0	2	3	1	2	3	1	0	14
ECADDES Home	1	1	0	3	1	0	1	3	1	1	12
ECADDES School	1	1	0	3	1	0	1	3	1	1	12

Note. ACTeRS = ADHD Comprehensive Teacher Rating Scale; ADHD-V = ADHD Rating Scale-V; BASC-3 = Behavior Assessment System for Children: Third Edition; Brown ADD = Brown Attention-Deficit Disorder Scales; CBCL = Achenbach Child Behavior Checklist: Attention Deficit/Hyperactivity Problems DSM-Oriented scale; C-TRF = Achenbach Caregiver-Teacher Report Form: Attention Deficit/Hyperactivity Problems DSM-Oriented scale; Conners = Conners Rating Scales-Revised; ECADDES = Early Childhood Attention Deficit Disorders Evaluation Scale. Internal Consistency, Test-Retest and Inter-rater reliability coefficients were averaged in order to produce a quality point rating.

Conners Scales for broadband scales and the ECADDES and the Brown ADD Scales for narrowband scales. Selection of measures may wish to involve consideration of these quality indicator scores along with the purpose of the assessment. Further, some measures (e.g., ADHD-V) had strong psychometric properties, but did not differentiate scores for children under 6 years of age from the overall school-age sample. Consequently, these scales scored lower on the quality indicators despite strong psychometric properties overall.

Summary

Evaluation of scale is a complex process that involves an interaction between the psychometric and practical utility of the scale. Although most manuals reviewed in this study provided sufficient evidence of reliability and validity for ages 5 years and older, most provided less detail about psychometric data with preschoolers. In many cases, psychometric information relevant to assessment with preschoolers was presented but was grouped together with data from other age groups (e.g., 4–11). For behavior rating scales to be helpful for assessment of preschoolers, more detailed information of the psychometric properties of these scales with this population is necessary and it is incumbent upon publishers to provide it.

There is a high rate of clinical referrals of preschool children with a range of disruptive behaviors; however, clinicians face pragmatic issues, including a lack of a direct method to assess preschool children's behavior (Wakschlag et al., 2005). In light of limited data on psychometric properties of rating scales for children younger than 5 years of age, it is recommended that clinicians consider rating scales in their assessment of preschool children in addition to methods such as direct observation. Furthermore, because the scales reviewed in this study differed in terms of various special features (e.g., validity scales, clinical norms), clinicians should carefully consider the match between the purpose of the assessment and the instrument used.

While the information gathered and examined in this review may be helpful to the researcher and the practitioner, it is not without limitations. First, the scales reviewed were ones that met our search and inclusionary criteria. As such, there is the possibility that there are other measures used in practice that clinicians and researchers find valuable. We encourage consideration of some of the variables discussed in this review as it pertains to preschool age children. Second, we reviewed scales based on the published data that would be available to researchers and practitioners in the manual that accompanies the scale. Additional data as to the psychometrics of the measures may be available in published and non-published formats. Finally, while the quality indicator review was based on the model put forth by Klein (2014) in reviewing scales for Autism Spectrum Disorders (ASD) and is built upon acceptable standards for psychometrics for screening, the model has not been replicated for use with ADHD, and as such, it would be important for researchers and practitioners to make scale selection based on criteria that are important to them.

Practical Implications

As noted above, a high rate of preschool referrals and a dearth of normative data for preschoolers might pose significant problems for clinicians, educators, and parents in providing care for young children. This study outlined the benefits of behavior rating scales that can be used to screen young children for ADHD. Based on the criteria and psychometric features examined, the best scale to use is highly dependent on the individual to be assessed as well as the purpose for assessment (e.g., diagnosis, progress monitoring, research). Clinicians and researchers may wish to consider the scales reviewed, their psychometric properties, and choose appropriately to assist in diagnosis and treatment planning for the preschool child referred for concerns about ADHD. If the objective of assessment is for progress monitoring of behaviors as a function of receipt of intervention, consideration of the stability of the measure may be warranted. If the purpose of the assessment is for diagnostic purposes in a research study, selection of a measure that links directly to DSM-5 criteria and has good cross-informant reliability may be important. With multiple measures of ADHD available for use with the preschool age population, selection of measurement approach should be an iterative process that incorporates multiple sources of data that consider evidence of reliability and validity of the measure for this age group.

References

Achenbach, T. M., & Rescorla, L. A. (2000). *Manual for the ASEBA preschool forms & profiles*. Burlington, VT: University of Vermont, Research Center for Children, Youth, & Families.

America Educational Research Association, American Psychological Association, & National Council Measurement Education. (2014). *Standards for educational and psychological testing*. Washington, DC: Author.

American Academy of Pediatrics. (2011). ADHD: Clinical practice guideline for the diagnosis, evaluation, and treatment of Attention-Deficit/Hyperactivity Disorder in children and adolescents. *Pediatrics, 128*(5), 1007–1022. Retrieved from https://doi.org/10.1542/peds.2011-2654

American Psychiatric Association. (1994). *Diagnostic and statistical manual of mental disorders* (4th ed.). Washington, DC: Author.

American Psychiatric Association. (2013). *Diagnostic and statistical manual of mental disorders* (5th ed.). Washington, DC: Author.

Anastasi, A. (1982). *Psychological testing* (5th ed.). New York, NY: The Macmillan Company.

Anastopoulos, A. D., & Shelton, T. L. (2001). *Assessing attention-deficit/hyperactivity disorder*. New York, NY: Kluwer Academic/Plenum Publishers.

Barkley, R. A. (1997). Attention-deficit hyperactivity disorder. In E. J. Mash & L. G. Terdal (Eds.), *Assessment of childhood disorders* (3rd ed.). New York, NY: Guilford Press.

Bendiksen, B., Svensson, E., Aase, H., Reichborn-Kjennerud, T., Friis, S., Myhre, A. M., & Zeiner, P. (2014). Co-Occurrence of ODD and CD in preschool children with symptoms of ADHD. *Journal of Attention Disorders, 1*, 1–12. doi:10.1177/1087054714538655

Breslau, J., Miller, E., Breslau, N., Bohnert, K., Lucia, V., & Schweitzer, J. (2009). The impact of early behavior disturbances on academic achievement in high school. *Pediatrics, 123*(6), 1472–1476. Retrieved from http://doi.org/10.1542/peds.2008-1406

Brown, T. E. (2001). *Brown Attention-Deficit Disorder Scales: For children and adolescents*. San Antonio, TX: The Psychological Corporation.

Bruchmüller, K., Margraf, J., & Schneider, S. (2012). Is ADHD diagnosed in accord with diagnostic criteria? Overdiagnosis and influence of client gender on diagnosis. *Journal of Consulting and Clinical Psychology, 80*(1), 128–138. doi:10.1037/a0026582

Bunte, T. L., Schoemaker, K., Hessen, D. J, van der Heijden, P. G. M., & Matthys, W. (2014). Stability and change of ODD, CD, and ADHD diagnosis in referred preschool children. *Journal of Abnormal Child Psychology, 42*(7), 1213–1224. Retrieved from https://doi.org/10.1007/s10802-014-9869-6

Burns, G. L., Boe, B., Walsh, J. A., Sommers-Flanagan, R., & Teegarden, L. (2001). A confirmatory factor analysis on the DSM-IV ADHD and ODD symptoms: What is the best model for the organization of these symptoms? *Journal of Abnormal Child Psychology, 29*, 339–349. Retrieved from https://doi.org/10.1023/A:1010314030025

Campbell S. B., Halperin J. M., & Sonuga-Barke E. J. S. (2014). A developmental perspective on attention-deficit/hyperactivity disorder (ADHD). In M. Lewis & K. Rudolph (Eds.), *Handbook of developmental psychopathology*. Springer: Boston, MA.

Chezan, L. C., Kratochwill, T. R., Terjesen, M. D., & Nguyen, K. V. H. (2017). Measuring outcomes in schools. In M. Terjesen & M. Thielking (Eds.), *Handbook of Australian School Psychology: International Research, Practice and Policy* (pp. 663–689). New York: Springer.

Chronis-Tuscano, A., Molina, B. G., Pelham, W. E., Applegate, B., Dahlke, A., Overmyer, M., & Lahey, B. B. (2010). Very early predictors of adolescent depression and suicide attempts in children with attention-deficit/hyperactivity disorder. *Archives of General Psychiatry, 67*(10), 1044–1051. doi:10.1001/archgenpsychiatry.2010.127

Conners, C. K. (2009). *Conners early childhood*. North Tonawanda, NY: Multi-Health Systems.

Connor, D. F. (2002). Preschool attention deficit hyperactivity disorder: A review of prevalence, diagnosis, neurobiology, and stimulant treatment. *Developmental and Behavioral Pediatrics, 23*(1S), S1–S9. doi:10.1097/00004703-200202001-00002

Curchack-Lichtin, J. T., Chacko, A., & Halperin, J. M. (2014). Changes in ADHD symptom endorsement: Preschool to school age. *Journal of Abnormal Child Psychology, 42*, 993–1004. Retrieved from https://doi.org/10.1007/s10802-013-9834-9

Danielson, M. L., Visser, S. N., Gleason, M. M., Peacock, G., Claussen, A. H., & Blumberg, S. J. (2017). A national profile of attention-deficit hyperactivity disorder diagnosis and treatment among U.S. children aged 2 to 5 years. *Journal of Developmental & Behavioral Pediatrics, 38*(7), 455–464. doi:10.1097/DBP.0000000000000477

De Los Reyes, A., Augenstein, T. M., Wang, M., Thomas, S. A., Drabick, D. A. G., Burgers, D. E., & Rabinowitz, J. (2015). The validity of the multi-informant approach to assessing child and adolescent mental health. *Psychological Bulletin, 141*(4), 858–900.

De Los Reyes, A., & Kazdin, A. E. (2005). Informant discrepancies in the assessment of childhood psychopathology: A critical review, theoretical framework, and recommendations for further study. *Psychological Bulletin, 131*(4), 483.

Demaray, M. K., Elting, J., & Schaefer, K. (2003). Assessment of attention-deficit/hyperactivity disorder (ADHD): A comparative evaluation of five, commonly used, published rating scales. *Psychology in the Schools, 40*, 341–361. doi:10.1002/pits.10112

Demaray, M. K., Scahefer, K., DeLong, L. K. (2003). Attention-deficit/hyperactivity disorder (ADHD): A national survey of training and current assessment practices in the schools. *Psychology in the Schools, 40*, 583–597. doi:10.1002/pits.10129

Diamantopoulou, S., Rydell, A., Thorell, L. B., & Bohlin, G. (2007). Impact of executive functioning and symptoms of attention deficit hyperactivity disorder on children's peer relations and school performance. *Developmental Neuropsychology, 32*(1), 521–542. doi:10.1080/87565640701360981 Top of Form

DuPaul, G. J., & Stoner, G. (2014). *ADHD in the schools: Assessment and intervention strategies*. New York, NY: Guilford Press.Bottom of Form

DuPaul, G. J., Power, T. J., Anastopoulos, A.D., & Reid, R. (2016). *Attention-deficit/hyperactivity disorder rating scale 5: Checklist, norms and clinical interpretation*. New York, NY: Guilford Press.

Egger, H. L., Kondo, D., & Angold, A. (2006). The epidemiology and diagnostic issues in preschool attention-deficit/hyperactivity disorder: A review. *Infants & Young Children. 19*(2), 109–122.

Hammill, D. D., Brown, L., & Bryant, B. R. (1994). *A consumer's guide to tests in print* (2nd ed.). Austin, TX: PRO-ED.

Healey, D. M., Miller, C. J., Castelli, K. L., Marks, D. J., & Haleprin, J. M. (2008). The impact of impairment criteria on rates of ADHD diagnoses in preschoolers. *Journal of Abnormal Child Psychology, 36*, 771–778. doi:10.1007/s10802-007-9209-1

Hinshaw, S. P., & Nigg, J. T. (1999). Behavior rating scales in the assessment of disruptive behavior problems in childhood. In D. Shaffer, C. P. Lucas, & J. E.

Richters (Eds.), *Diagnostic assessment in child and adolescent psychopathology* (pp. 91–126). New York, NY: Guilford Press.

Kazdin, A. E. (2002). *Research design in clinical psychology* (4th ed.). Boston: Allyn & Bacon.

Klein, A. (2014). *Examining the psychometric properties of measures of autism-spectrum disorders.* Retrieved from ProQuest Dissertations Publishing. (UMI Number: 3579772)

Magnússon, P., Smári, J., Sigurðardóttir, D., Baldursson, G., Sigmundsson, J., Kristjánsson, K.,... Guðmundsson, Ó. Ó. (2006). Validity of self-report and informant rating scales of adult ADHD symptoms in comparison with a semi-structured diagnostic interview. *Journal of Attention disorders, 9*(3), 494–503.

Mahone, E. M. (2005). Measurement of attention and related functions in the preschool child. *Mental Retardation Developmental Disabilities Research Review; 11*, 216–225.

Mandal, R. L., Olmi, D. J., & Wilczynski, S. M. (1999). Behavior rating scales: Concordance between multiple informants in the diagnosis of attention-deficit/hyperactivity disorder. *Journal of Attention Disorders, 3*, 97–103. doi:10.1177/108705479900300204

Manning, S. C., & Miller, D. C. (2001). Identifying ADHD Subtypes using the Parent and Teacher Rating Scales of the Behavior Assessment Scale for Children. Journal of Attention Disorders, 5(1), 41–51. https://doi.org/10.1177/108705470100500104

McCarney, S. B. (1995). *Early Childhood attention deficit disorders evaluation scale (ECADDES)*. Columbia, MO: Hawthorne Educational Services.

McCarney, S. B., & Arthaud, T. J. (1994). *Attention Deficit Disorder Evaluation Scale* (4th ed.). Columbia, MO: Hawthorne.

McGough, J. J., & McCracken, J. T. (2000). Assessment of attention deficit hyperactivity disorder: A review of recent literature. *Current Opinion in Pediatrics, 12*, 319–324. doi:10.1097/00008480-200008000-00006

Merikangas, K. R., He, J.-P., Brody, D., Fisher, P. W., Bourdon, K., & Koretz, D. S. (2010). Prevalence and treatment of mental disorders among U.S. children in the 2001–2004 NHANES. *Pediatrics, 125*(1), 75–81. Retrieved from http://doi.org/10.1542/peds.2008-2598

Merrell, K. W. (2007). *Behavioral, social, and emotional assessment of children and adolescents* (3rd ed.). New York, NY: Lawrence Erlbaum Associates.

Messick, S. (1995). Validity of psychological assessment: Validation of inferences from persons' responses and performances as scientific inquiry into score meaning. *American Psychologist, 50*(9), 741–749. doi:10.1037/0003-066X.50.9.741

Pastor, P. N., & Reuben, C. A. (2005). Racial and ethnic differences in ADHD and LD in young school-age children: Parental reports in the national health interview survey. *Public Health Reports, 120*(4), 383–392.

Pastor, P. N., Reuben, C. A., Duran, C. R., & Hawkins, L. D. (2015). Association between diagnosed ADHD and selected characteristics among children aged 4–17 years: United States, 2011–2013. *NCHS data brief, no. 201.* Hyattsville, MD: National Center for Health Statistics.

Pelham, W. E., Fabiano, G. A., & Massetti, G. M. (2005). Evidence-based assessment of attention deficit hyperactivity disorder in children and adolescents. *Journal of Clinical Child and Adolescent Psychology, 34,* 449–476. doi:10.1207/s15374424jccp3403_5

Posner, K., Melvin, G. A., Murray, D. W., Gugga, S. S., Fisher, P., Skrobala, A., & Greenhill, L. L. (2007). Clinical presentation of attention-deficit/hyperactivity disorder in preschool children: The preschoolers with attention-deficit/hyperactivity disorder treatment study (PATS) *Journal of Child and Adolescent Psychopharmacology, 17*(5), 547–562.

Power, T. J., & Ikeda, M.J. (1996). The clinical utility of behavior rating scales: Comments on the diagnostic assessment of ADHD. *Journal of School Psychology, 34,* 379–385. doi:10.1016/S0022-4405(96)00023-4

Reid, R., & Maag, J. W. (1994). How many fidgets in a pretty much: A critique of behavior rating scales for identifying students with ADHD. *Journal of School Psychology, 32,* 339–354. doi:10.1016/0022-4405(94)90032-9

Reid, R., Riccio, C. A., Kessler, R. H., DuPaul, G. J., Power, T. J., Anastopoulos, A. D., ... Noll, M. (2000). Gender and ethnicity differences in ADHD as assessed by behavior ratings. *Journal of Emotional and Behavioral Disorders, 8,* 38–48. doi:10.1177/106342660000800105

Reynolds, C., & Kamphaus, R. (2015). *Behavioral assessment system for children* (3rd ed.). Bloomington, MN: Pearson Clinical Assessment Group.

Riddle, M. A., Yershova, K., Lazzaretto, D., Paykina, N., Yenokyan, G., Greenhill, L., ... Posner, K. (2013). The preschool attention-deficit/hyperactivity disorder treatment study (PATS) 6-year follow-up. *Journal of the American Academy of Child and Adolescent Psychiatry, 52*(3), 264–278.e2. http://doi.org/10.1016/j.jaac.2012.12.007

Ryser, G. R., Campbell, H. L., & Miller, B. K. (2010). Confirmatory factor analysis of the scales for diagnosing attention deficit hyperactivity disorder (scales). *Educational and Psychological Measurement, 70*(5), 844–857. doi:10.1177/0013164410366696

Sattler, J. M. (2014). *Foundations of behavioral, social, and clinical assessment of children* (6th ed.). San Diego, CA: Author.

Shapiro, E.S., & Heick, P.F. (2004). School psychologist assessment practices in the evaluation of students referred for social/behavioral/emotional problems. *Psychology in the Schools, 41*, 551–561. doi:10.1002/pits.10176

Shaw, M., Hodgkins, P., Caci, H., Young, S., Kahle, J., Woods, A. G., & Arnold, L. E. (2012). A systematic review and analysis of long-term outcomes in attention deficit hyperactivity disorder: Effects of treatment and non-treatment. *BMC Medicine, 10*, 99. Retrieved from http://doi.org/10.1186/1741-7015-10-99

Shelton, T. L., & Barkley, R. A. (1993). Assessment of attention-deficit hyperactivity disorder in young children. In D. J. Willis & J. L. Culbertson (Eds.), *Testing young children: A reference guide for developmental, psychoeducational, and psychosocial assessments* (pp. 290–318). Austin, TX: PRO-ED.

Smith, B. L. (2011). ADHD among preschoolers. *Monitor on Psychology, 42*(7). Retrieved from http://www.apa.org/monitor/2011/07-08/adhd.aspx

Smith, K. G., & Corkum, P. (2007). Systematic review of measures used to diagnose attention-deficit/hyperactivity disorder in research on preschool children. *Topics in Early Childhood Special Education, 27*(3), 164–173. doi:10.1177/02711214070270030701

Steinhoff, K. W., Lerner, M., Kapilinsky. A., Kotkin, R., Wigal, S., Steinberg-Epstein, R., ... Swanson J. M. (2006). Attention-deficit/hyperactivity disorder. In J. L. Luby (Ed.) *Handbook of Preschool Mental Health: Development, Disorders, and Treatment.* (pp. 63–79). New York, NY: Guilford Press.

Terjesen, M.D., & Kurasaki, R. (2009). Assessment and intervention for ADHD in early childhood. In F. Rubinson, B. Mowder, & A. Yasik, (Eds.), *Evidence-based practice in infant and early childhood psychology.* New York, NY: Wiley.

Thomas, R., Sanders, S., Doust, J., Beller, E., & Glasziou, P. (2015). Prevalence of attention-deficit/hyperactivity disorder: A systematic review and meta-analysis. *Pediatrics, 135*, e994–e1001. doi:10.1542/peds.2014-3482

Thorell, L. B., & Rydell, A. M. (2008). Behaviour problems and social competence deficits associated with symptoms of attention-deficit/hyperactivity disorder: Effects of age and gender. *Child: Care, Health and Development, 34*(5), 584–595. doi:10.1111/j.1365-2214.2008.00869.x

Tobin, R. M., Schneider, W. J., & Landau, S. (2014). Best practices in the assessment of youth with attention deficit hyperactivity disorder within a multitiered services framework. In P. Harrison & A. Thomas (Eds.), *Best practices in school psychology: Data-based and collaborative decision making* (pp. 391–404). Bethesda, MD: National Association of School Psychologists.

Ullmann, R. K., Sleator, E. K., & Sprague, R. L. (2000). *ACTeRS teacher, parent, and self-report forms manual* (2nd ed.). Champaign, IL: MetriTech.

Visser, S. N., Danielson, M. L., Bitsko, R. H., Holbrook, J. R., Kogan, M. D., Ghandour, R. M., ... Blumberg, S. J. (2014). Trends in the parent-report of health care provider diagnosed and medicated ADHD: United States, 2003–2011. *Journal of the American Academy of Child and Adolescent Psychiatry, 53*(1), 34–46.e2. Retrieved from http://doi.org/10.1016/j.jaac.2013.09.001

Visser, S. N., Bitsko, R. H., Danielson, M. L., Ghandour, R. M., Blumberg, S. J., Schieve, L. A., ... Cuffe, S. P. (2015). Treatment of attention-deficit/hyperactivity disorder among children with special health care needs. *The Journal of Pediatrics, 166*(6), 1423–1430.e2. Retrieved from https://doi.org/10.1016/j.jpeds.2015.02.018

Volpe, R. J., & DuPaul, G. J. (2001). Assessment with brief behavior rating scales. In J. J. W. J. Andrews, H. Janzen, & D. Saklofske (Eds.), *Handbook of psychoeducational assessment: Ability, achievement, and behavior in children* (pp. 357–387). San Diego, CA: Academic Press.

Wåhlstedt, C., Thorell, L. B., & Bohlin, G. (2008). ADHD symptoms and executive function impairment: Early predictors of later behavioral problems. *Developmental Neuropsychology, 33*, 160–178.

Wakschlag, L. S., Leventhal, B. L., Briggs-Gowan, M. J., Danis, B., Keenan, K., Hill, C. & Carter, A. S. (2005). Defining the "disruptive" in preschool behavior: What diagnostic observation can teach us. *Clinical Child and Family Psychology Review, 8*(3), 183–201. doi:10.1007/s10567-005-6664-5

Weyandt, L. L. (2007). *An ADHD primer* (2nd ed.). Mahwah, NJ: Lawrence Erlbaum Associates.

Children's Adjustment to Kindergarten: Predictions from Mother-Child Emotional Availability and Children's Narratives Prior to School Entry

Jun Wang, Hannah Wurster, Shauna Skillern Fisher, Kate Shepard, Jennifer Gerber Moné, and Zeynep Biringen

Abstract

The transition into kindergarten is a momentous and challenging task for young children. Although this challenge requires the acquisition of new academic skills, it also requires certain social and emotional competencies, which can strongly affect how well children adjust to formal schooling. Mother-child emotional availability (EA) and children's narratives were assessed prior to the start of school, and children's social and emotional outcomes were evaluated at the start of the kindergarten year and at the end. Results indicated that mother-child EA (assessed during the prekindergarten year) was predictive of fewer child social problems in kindergarten; on the other hand, children's ability to formulate cognitively complex narratives in which they are affectively engaged was predictive of child social competence. Furthermore, as would be expected, children's language ability was associated with the quality of children's narratives. However, children's narratives did not serve as a mediator between mother-child EA and children's social-emotional outcomes. Finally, social problems and social competence demonstrated strong stability across the school year. Findings are discussed in terms of intervention possibilities to promote children's social-emotional well-being as they make the transition to school.

***Keywords:* emotional availability, narratives, socioemotional competence, school readiness, mother-child relationship**

Entering kindergarten is a monumental transition for children and their families. During this period, children gain increased independence and responsibility in many arenas of their lives (Whiting & Edwards, 1988). The formal school system presents children with new expectations, including compliance with formal rules, cooperation with peers, formal routines, and perseverance at new and difficult cognitive tasks. At the same time, parental demands for rule compliance and personal responsibility also increase during this developmental period (Gralinski & Kopp, 1993). Additionally, the school system's focus on academic advancement and cognitive skills differs from many children's prior experiences in childcare settings, preschool, or at home where exploration, play, and socialization may have been emphasized more (Rimm-Kaufman & Pianta, 2000). The transition into kindergarten imposes many new and challenging demands on children, requiring them to flexibly adjust to the requirements of this new setting. Therefore, it is important to examine the factors that contribute to socioemotional adjustment to kindergarten.

Emotional Availability in Mother-Child Relationships Prior to School Entry

Emotional availability (EA) is the capacity of a dyad to share a healthy emotional connection and to enjoy a mutually fulfilling relationship (Biringen & Easterbrooks, 2012). Emotional availability (EA) derives from attachment theory (Bowlby, 1969; 1980), but it serves as a "second generation" conceptualization of attachment because it expands the theoretical concepts to include aspects of a caregiver-child relationship other than sensitivity of the caregiver (Biringen, 2008; Biringen, Robinson, & Emde, 1998). EA also includes qualities such as emotional expression, guidance of learning, autonomy support, and absence of hostility (Biringen, Derscheid, Vliegen, Closson, & Easterbrooks, 2014). In addition, EA considers how the characteristics and behaviors of a child contribute to the quality of the relationship. Thus, EA describes broader qualities of an emotional and dyadic relationship between an adult and a child (Biringen, 2008; Biringen et al., 2014).

Emotional availability consists of six dimensions, four of which refer to the adult's behavior and emotional expressions, and two of which refer to the child's. Adult sensitivity refers to the capacity of the adult to maintain an appropriate affect and respond effectively to the child's cues. Structuring describes the adult's ability to lead the child to a more sophisticated level of understanding. Non-intrusiveness refers to the adult's tendency to follow the child's lead and permit age-appropriate levels of autonomy and independence. Non-hostility describes the adult's ability to regulate his or her emotions and refrain from treating the child in a hostile manner. Child responsiveness consists of the child's tendency to respond positively to the adult's bids, while also maintaining age-appropriate levels of autonomy. Finally, child involvement is the child's behavior and communication that draws the adult into the play and collaborates with the adult to construct an elaborative storyline (Biringen, 2008; Biringen et al., 1998).

The EA Scales (Biringen, 2008; Biringen et al., 1998) have been used to examine how EA between a mother and a child predicts the child's socioemotional school readiness (Biringen et al., 2005). In a paper using the current sample, Biringen and colleagues (2005) found that EA predicted children's adjustment to kindergarten. An EA sub-composite (sum of all maternal and child EA dimensions, not including sensitivity) was computed. Then, in multiple regression analyses, the researchers first entered the extent of preschool experience and language competence. At the second step they entered maternal sensitivity, and in the final step, they entered the EA sub-composite. In each multiple regression equation, the EA sub-composite predicted child school outcomes (including direct observations of child aggression and victimization, teacher reports of positive skills and behavior problems, as well as child reports of loneliness) even after controlling for maternal sensitivity. These results suggested the significance of the larger EA concept above and beyond just a focus on maternal sensitivity. Further, other studies also have found that higher EA predicts lower internalizing and externalizing behaviors during the transition to kindergarten among a high-risk, ethnically diverse sample (Kang, 2005).

Children's Ability to Formulate Narratives Prior to School Entry

In his formulation of attachment theory, John Bowlby (1969; 1980) proposed that high quality parenting during infancy creates a bond that both protects infants and grants them a secure base from which to explore their environment. Positive parenting styles with the primary caregiver can help to predict children's adjustment and competence later in life. Children who enjoy secure and positive emotional relationships with their caregivers show more positive emotional expressions, have better peer relationships, and are seen as more attractive by their peers than their less fortunate counterparts (Ladd & Profilet, 1996; Sroufe, 2000). They are also more likely to process social experiences with a positive bias and to reflect on their relational experiences with more coherence and flexibility (Dykas & Cassidy, 2011; George, Kaplan, & Main, 1984). Thus, children's early attachment relationships not only predict their socio-emotional functioning, but also influence how these children process and represent their social worlds even into adulthood. Such processing of the social world can be assessed through the way in which children tell fictional stories, often referred to as "narratives" (Emde, Wolf, & Oppenheim, 2003; Laible, Carlo, Torquati, & Ontai, 2004). Children who experience sensitive parenting have been found to tell narratives that are coherent and contain prosocial content, whereas children who experience harsh parenting tell narratives with aggressive themes (Laible et al., 2004). We were specifically interested in whether children's cognitively complex narratives told in engaging and emotionally positive ways would be predictive of their future relationships in school. Because the children in this study have not yet started kindergarten and are less than or equal to 5 years of age, we wanted to have a sense of both their words as well as their actions as they tell stories, and thus evaluated the narratives directly from videos.

Although mother-child relationship quality and children's quality of narratives may directly affect their social adjustment once they enter school, it is also a possibility that the complexity, engagement, and positive quality of children's narratives may mediate the relation between parenting behaviors and their socioemotional functioning (Shields, Ryan, & Cicchetti, 2001; Solomonica-Levi, Yirmiya, Erel, Samat, & Oppenheim, 2001; Stadelman, Perren, von Wyl, & von Klitzing, 2007). Therefore, it is possible that children's observed relational experiences (i.e., EA) prior to school influence their adjustment to kindergarten through the way in which they are able to think about and feel about their relationships (i.e., narratives).

Language

Children's ability to express themselves through narratives depends, in part, on their expressive and receptive language skills, and children with higher language competence are more likely to produce coherent narratives (Fiorentino & Howe, 2004). Furthermore, language also contributes to social abilities relevant to school readiness. Children with higher receptive language skills have been rated by teachers to be more socially, physically, and academically prepared for kindergarten (Fiorentino & Howe, 2004). Additionally, children with a speech/language impairment have been found to be at risk for certain social problems, such as lower self-control, limited assertiveness, and greater internalizing symptoms (McCabe & Meller, 2004). Another study demonstrated that language difficulties at the time of school entry predicted lower social competence during kindergarten (Justice, Bowles, Pence Turnbull, & Skibbe, 2009). Therefore, language abilities may play a role in both children's expression of narratives and in their readiness for kindergarten. The current study will examine language as a potential predictor of children's narrative skills, thus confounding the relations among mother-child EA, children's narratives, and children's socioemotional outcomes.

Present Study

We expect that the overall quality of parent-child relationships plays a direct role in children's adjustment to kindergarten. In addition, we expect that, in line with attachment theory, children's early caregiving experiences set the tone for their behavior toward new social partners at school (Bowlby, 1969; Bretherton, 1990). Therefore, the present study examines whether mother-child emotional availability predicts children's socioemotional adjustment to kindergarten, as well as whether children's ability to formulate complex and affectively toned narratives in which they are fully engaged may impact children's actual relationships in kindergarten. We additionally ask if EA indirectly predicts children's adjustment by way of children's narratives.

To address these questions related to emotional availability, in the main analyses, we chose to use a latent construct of overall EA in the mother-child relationship, which (to our knowledge) has not been previously featured in the literature on emotional availability. In addition, the other main variables in the study were also studied as latent constructs in order to examine how dyadic mother-child relationships prior to kindergarten entry predict children's narrative stories, and how both predict child adjustment during the kindergarten year.

The present study will seek to answer:
1. Does EA predict children's social competence and social problems during the transition to kindergarten?
2. Does the quality of children's narratives mediate the relationships between EA and child social competence and social problems during the transition to kindergarten?

3. Does EA predict children's social competence and social problems in the later stages of kindergarten adjustment?
4. Does the quality of children's narratives mediate the relationship between EA and child social competence and social problems in the later stages of kindergarten adjustment?
5. Does language ability predict the quality of children's narratives?
6. Are children's social competence and social problems stable between the transition to kindergarten and the later stages of kindergarten adjustment?

We predict that EA will relate to children's socioemotional competence and socioemotional problems at both time points. We also predict that the quality and content of children's narratives will relate to children's socioemotional competence and problems. Further, we will test two theoretically-based hypotheses against one another in order to determine whether children's narratives serve as a mediator between EA and socioemotional outcomes or whether each is a unique and direct predictor. Finally, we expect that there would be intra-individual stability in social competence and social problems between the early stages and the later stages of kindergarten adjustment (see Figure 1 for the conceptual model of the constructs).

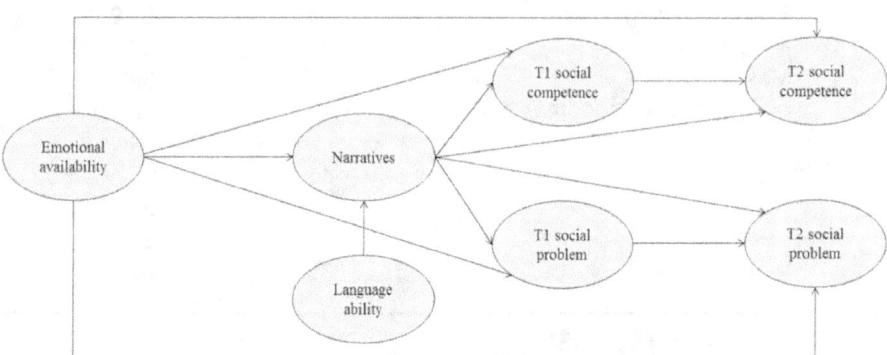

Figure 1. Conceptual structure model of the latent constructs.

Method
Participants

Participants were 57 mother-child pairs. Children were in preschool at the start of the study and were preparing to enter kindergarten in the fall. The sample was diverse in terms of educational level and occupational status of the families (see Table 1 for the demographics of the sample). The educational level of the

Table 1
Demographics of the Participants

Demographic variables	N	%
Gender	54	
Males	26	48.1
Females	28	51.9
Family Income	56	
under 5,000	1	1.8
5-10,000	2	3.6
10-15,000	1	1.8
20-30,000	10	17.9
30-50,000	18	32.1
over 50,000	24	42.9
Mother's Education	56	
7-11 years	1	1.8
high school	8	14.3
1-3 years college	19	33.9
4 years college	21	37.5
Master's degree	3	5.4
beyond Master's degree	4	7.1
Ethnic group	41	
Asian	1	2.4
Black	1	2.4
White	39	95.1

mothers ranged from those who completed middle school to those who completed master's degrees. There were 26 boys and 28 girls in the study. Caregivers reported on child ethnicity; 39 were Caucasian and 2 non-Caucasian (one of African American origin and one of Asian origin), and 13 parents did not respond to the question.

Measures

Narratives. The MacArthur Story Stem Battery (MSSB; Bretherton, Oppenheim, Emde, & MacArthur Narrative Working Group, 2003) is a tool used to assess children's narratives about the social world. In this task, children are asked to complete an emotionally charged story using words and play action. In this task, the researcher first tells a practice story stem to teach the child the task. Then, the researcher tells nine test story stems that include a form of relational conflict. For each stem, the child is asked to finish the story. Given our interest in understanding how emotionally and cognitively engaged the children could be in telling these stories, we developed three 5-point scales to score the narratives: (a) engagement and attention; (b) complexity of the representations; and (c) affective tone of the representations. Given the young age of these children and because we were interested in children's facial and bodily expressions of engagement and affect in the story-telling activity, we scored directly from the videos.

Engagement and attention refers to the extent to which the child is enthusiastic and willing to participate in the story-telling task. If a child showed a great deal of enthusiasm and pleasure in participating in the activity, the child received a 5. If a child seemed involved in the story-telling activity but often asked questions that took him off the activity or tried to include contexts in the story that did not belong, the child received a 3. If a child was unwilling to participate in the activity, disinterested, or distracted by other stimuli, the child received a 1. A low score of 1 was also given to a child who displayed a positive effect, but not towards the designated activity.

Cognitive complexity of narratives refers to the elaborative nature of the plot. If a child could take a simple story beginning and turn it into a coherently elaborated and positively creative story, the child received a 5. If the child responded to the story in a relevant and coherent way but did not elaborate much, or the responses were not generally positively creative, the child received a 3. If a child did not elaborate spontaneously, needed a great deal of coaxing and persuasion by the examiner, and/or told stories with impoverished plots, the child received a 1. Also, a 1 was given to a child who elaborated in irrelevant or disorganized ways so that there was significant incoherence in the storylines. If a child described irrational consequences or traumatic experiences, this was considered a disorganized and incoherent story because the plot was not positively creative.

Affective tone of the narratives refers to the emotional quality of the stories. If a child described relationships as generally positive and rewarding and appeared to expect good things to happen in relationships, the child received a 5. If a child described positive relationships, but the tone was more neutral or low key and less affectionate or loving, the child received a 3. If a child described relationships that were threatening, abandoning, abusing, or destructive and/or people that were uncaring, unpleasant, or victimizing, the child received a 1. If the child exhibited significant avoidance of affective themes or negative issues but was not entirely negative in affective tone, then the child received a 2. For example, a child receiving a 2 might have said, "let's sleep," on a regular basis throughout a narrative. Two assistants independently rated the first 10 cases directly from the videotapes (using both verbal and nonverbal cues) and achieved intraclass correlations of .80 on each scale. For these 10 cases, where there was disagreement of two or more points, the coders' conferenced scores were used. Each coder then rated half the remaining sample. The last author routinely conducted random checks of the sample and was in agreement (within 1 point) on nine out of 10 cases; no additional conferencing was therefore conducted.

Emotional Availability (EA) Scales. Mother-child interaction videos were coded using the third edition of the Emotional Availability Scales, Early Childhood Version (EAS; Biringen et al., 1998). The full 20-minute play interaction was coded together to obtain EA scores for "overall play." This assessment consists of four adult scales—sensitivity, structuring, non-intrusiveness, and non-hostility—and two child scales—responsiveness and involvement. Sensitivity was coded on a 7-point scale ranging from 1 (*nonoptimal*) to 8 (*optimal*) and the other dimensions of adult EA were coded in the third edition on 5-point scales ranging from 1 (*nonoptimal*) to 5 (*optimal*). The child scales were coded on 7-point scales, ranging from 1 (*nonoptimal*) to 7 (*optimal*).

The EAS has been used in numerous studies, both nationally and internationally (Biringen et al., 2014). They have high inter-rater reliability and correlations with child-mother attachment for school-age children (Biringen et al., 2014). For this sample, the fourth and fifth authors were trained centrally by the last author, the developer of the scales. After achieving reliability through training, they double-coded the first 10 cases and achieved intraclass correlations of at least .80 on each of the six EA dimensions for these cases. After this reliability check, the fourth author coded the remainder of the sample.

Child Behavior Scale. The Child Behavior Scale (CBS; Ladd & Profilet, 1996) is a 59-item measure that assesses aggressive, withdrawn, and prosocial behaviors in children. Each item describes a child behavior or characteristic; for example, one item reads, "taunts and teases classmates." Teachers were instructed to rate how well each item applies to an individual child using a 3-point scale ranging from 1 (*does not apply*) to 2 (*applies sometimes*) and 3 (*certainly applies*). Items are grouped into six subscales: aggressive with peers (7 items), prosocial with peers (10 items), excluded by peers (7 items), asocial with peers (7 items), anxious/fearful in social contexts (9 items), and hyperactive-distractible (4 items). In previous studies, Cronbach's alpha for the six subscales ranged from .77 to .96. Subscales correlated moderately with observational measures of child behavior and highly with other teacher-report measures of child behavior (Ladd & Profilet, 1996). In the current study, Cronbach's alphas for CBS subscales ranged from .74 for anxious/fearful in social contexts at Time 1 to .91 for aggressive with peers at both Time 1 and Time 2.

Teacher-Child Rating Scale. The Teacher-Child Rating Scale (TCRS) is a teacher-report measure of children's competencies and behavior problems at school (Hightower et al., 1986). The scale consists of 38 items. Eighteen items describe problem behaviors and are coded on a 5-point scale ranging from 1 (*not a problem*) to 5 (*very serious problem*). The remaining 20 items measure child competencies and are coded on a 5-point scale ranging from 1 (*not at all*) to 5 (*very well*). Items load onto seven subscales: conduct problems, learning problems, shy/anxious problems, frustration tolerance, work habits, assertive social skills, and peer sociability. Each of these seven scales were comprised of 5 items. The first three subscales form the behavior problems aggregate, and the remaining four form the competence aggregate. Scores are calculated for each of the 7 subscales, as well as for the 2 aggregates. Cronbach's alphas for the TCRS subscales range from .85 to .95 (Hightower et al., 1986), and the TCRS correlates with other meaningful school-based indices, including other behavior checklists, grades, and scores on standardized tests (Trickett, McBride-Change, & Putman, 1994). In the current study, Cronbach's alphas for TCRS subscales ranged from .77 for shy/anxious problems at Time 2 to .95 for work habits at Time 2.

Social Skills Rating System. The Social Skills Rating System teacher version (SSRS-T; Gresham & Elliott, 1990) assesses social skills, problem behaviors, and academic competence. The SSRS-T consists of 30 items coded on a 3-point scale ranging from 0 (*never*) to 2 (*often*). Items are grouped into three subscales with 10 items each: cooperation (e.g., "follows your direction), assertion (e.g., "invites others to join in activities"), and self-control (e.g., "responds appropriately when pushed or hit by other children"). Previous studies using the SSRS-T demonstrated its internal consistency and discriminant validity (Van der Oord et al., 2005). In the current study, Cronbach's alphas for SSRS-T subscales ranged from .84 for Cooperation at Time 1 to .91 for Cooperation at Time 2.

Student-Teacher Relationship Scale. The Student-Teacher Relationship Scale (STRS; Pianta, 2001) assesses teachers' perceptions of their relationship with an individual student. For example, one item reads, "this child easily becomes angry at me." The STRS consists of 28 items that are scored on a 5-point scale ranging from 1 (*definitely does not apply*) to 5 (*definitely applies*). Items are categorized into three subscales: conflict, closeness, and dependency, with 12 items comprising the conflict scale, 11 items comprising the closeness scale, and 5 items comprising the dependency scale. Previous studies using the STRS have demonstrated its reliability and predictive, concurrent, and construct validity (Birch & Ladd, 1997; Hamre & Pianta, 2001; Howes, Phillipsen, & Peisner-Feinberg, 2000; Murray & Murray, 2004; Pianta, 2001; Rudasill & Rimm-Kaufmann, 2009). In the current study, Cronbach's alphas for STRS subscales ranged from .58 for Dependency at Time 2 to .88 for Conflict at Time 2.

Language assessments. This study used the Expressive One-Word Picture Vocabulary Test (EOWPVT) and Receptive One-Word Picture Vocabulary (ROWPVT) tests in order to assess child language ability. In the expressive test, a child is shown 190 color illustrations depicting an action, object, or concept, and asked to name each illustration. In the receptive test, the examiner speaks a word and presents four color pictures. The child then points to the picture that illustrates the meaning of the word.

The ROWPVT also contains 190 items. The respective manuals present transformations from raw to standard scores for both tests. Internal consistency was determined through Cronbach's coefficient alphas and split-half reliability on both the Expressive and Receptive tests. Coefficients for the receptive test ranged from 0.95 to 0.98, and split-half reliability scores ranged from 0.97 to 0.99. Coefficient alphas for the expressive test ranged from 0.93 to 0.98, and split-half coefficients ranged from 0.96 to 0.99. Concurrent validity tests were conducted on both the expressive and receptive tests. The tests have been shown to be highly correlated with other vocabulary tests, such as the WISC-III and the EVT (Brownell, 2000).

Procedure

Data were collected during the spring/summer months before kindergarten entry (prekindergarten phase) as well as during the kindergarten year (kindergarten phase). To recruit families, parents were approached during registration for kindergarten at two elementary schools serving the most socioeconomically diverse populations in a small college town. They were told about the Transition to Elementary School Project, a study to examine family/child factors affecting successful adjustment to kindergarten, and asked for contact information. All parents coming in for kindergarten registration were interested in future contact regarding the study. When contacted by phone, over 80% of parents consented to participate.

Prekindergarten phase. Data for the prekindergarten phase were conducted in our laboratory. After explaining the study in detail and obtaining informed consent through a procedure approved by the university's Institutional Review Board, a research assistant started administering measures. First, to assess EA, the mother and child were instructed to sit at a table and play with an Etch-A-Sketch. They were told to each use a dial in order to work together and "sketch" two pictures. Models of a house and boat were placed in front of the dyad. Following a 5-minute period, the research assistant replaced the Etch-A-Sketch with Playmobile toys with a medieval theme. The research assistant instructed the pair to "play as you normally would with these toys." At the end of 15 minutes, the researcher returned and asked the pair to clean up the toys. The Emotional Availability Scales (Version 3; Biringen et al., 1998) were used to code the 20 minutes of mother-child play.

Following the play period, a research assistant administered the language assessments (Brownell, 2000) and play narratives (Bretherton et al., 2003) to the child while the mother was in another room down a long hallway being interviewed (children were shown where their mothers would be located). This was also videotaped.

Kindergarten phase. Data collection during the kindergarten phase occurred twice, once in the first month of the school year (Time 1), and then at the end of the second semester (Time 2). At each of these time points, teachers received packet of questionnaires for each target child. The packet consisted of the Child Behavior Scale (Ladd & Profilet, 1996), the Teacher-Child Rating Scale (Hightower et al., 1986), the Social Skills Rating System (Gresham & Elliott, 1990), and the Student-Teacher Relationship Scale (Pianta, 2001).

Results

Preliminary analyses

To understand the relations between the individual EA dimensions and children's behaviors, zero-order correlations were computed among all the observed variables. For brevity, rather than present all of these (49 × 49) correlations in tabular format, herein we summarize the significant findings. All correlations that are at $p < .05$ levels are noted here, but those that are at $p < .01$ levels are highlighted as *strongly* correlated. With respect to EA-language linkages, both maternal sensitivity and non-hostility are positively correlated with the child's expressive language competence, using both raw as well as standard scores. There are no significant correlations for raw or standard receptive language scores, however. With respect to the EA-narrative linkages, only the children's cognitive complexity of narratives is correlated with the dimensions of EA (i.e., maternal sensitivity, non-hostility, child responsiveness [strongly], and child involvement), suggesting it is this complexity that is most associated with mother-child EA. There are no correlations that reach significance between the EA dimensions and the other components of child narratives: affect tone or engagement/attention.

In terms of EA-CBS linkages at T1, maternal sensitivity is significantly negatively correlated with exclusion by peers. Maternal structuring is negatively correlated with aggression with peers and hyperactivity/distractibility and positively correlated with prosocial behaviors (strongly). Maternal non-hostility is negatively correlated significantly with aggression with peers and exclusion by peers. Child responsiveness is negatively correlated only with hyperactivity/distractibility. In terms of EA-CBS linkages at T2, maternal sensitivity is negatively correlated with aggression with peers and, once again, negatively correlated with exclusion by peers. Maternal structuring is strongly and negatively correlated with aggression with peers, exclusion by peers as well as with hyperactivity/distractibility. Maternal non-intrusiveness is positively correlated with prosocial behaviors. Maternal non-hostility is correlated negatively now only with aggression with peers. Child responsiveness and child involvement are negatively correlated with exclusion by peers and hyperactivity/distractibility, and child involvement is additionally negatively correlated with asocial behaviors.

In terms of EA-SSRS linkages at T1, maternal sensitivity is positively correlated with assertion and maternal structuring is strongly positively correlated with cooperation. At T2, maternal sensitivity is positively correlated with self-control and maternal structuring is positively correlated with both cooperation and self-control.

In terms of EA-TCRS linkages at T1, maternal sensitivity and maternal structuring and child responsiveness and child involvement are strongly negatively correlated with acting out and learning problems. In addition, maternal sensitivity is positively correlated with assertive social skills and strongly correlated with peer social skills. Maternal structuring is additionally correlated with peer social skills. At T2, maternal sensitivity is correlated positively only with peer social skills. Structuring continues to be positively correlated with peer social skills as well as negatively correlated with acting out and learning problems. Child responsiveness and child involvement continue to be correlated negatively with acting out, and now they are also correlated positively with peer social skills.

In terms of EA-STRS linkages at T1, sensitivity is negatively correlated with conflict and positively correlated with closeness. Maternal structuring is correlated negatively with conflict. Child responsiveness is correlated negatively with conflict and positively with closeness. At T2, only structuring is correlated negatively with conflict. Overall, these zero-order correlations are all in the expected direction and suggest a meaningful, holistic picture of mother-child EA (on both the parental and child sides) linked with positive child outcomes at both the transition to kindergarten as well as at the end of the kindergarten year. However, it is necessary to decrease the number of tests performed and also to present our model of linkages between these qualities. Next, path analysis with latent variables was conducted to examine whether and how prekindergarten EA, language ability, and narratives were associated with positive and negative child outcomes at both T1 and T2 during kindergarten.

Primary Analysis of EA-outcome Linkages

Analytical procedures. Model testing was performed using partial least squares (PLS) analysis with the SmartPLS Version 3.0 software (Ringle, Wende, & Becker, 2015). PLS is a variance-based approach (as distinct from covariance-based) used to investigate descriptive and predictive structural equation models involving latent (i.e., unobservable) variables indirectly measured by a block of observable indicators. PLS is especially suitable for prediction purposes (Fornell & Bookstein, 1982). It uses non-parametric procedures making no restrictive assumptions about the distributions of the data while estimating parameters (Frank & Miller, 1992). At any given moment, only a subset of the parameters are being estimated. Thus, PLS can handle complex models with many observed and latent variables efficiently. In addition, estimates generated by PLS are more stable than those generated by covariance-based SEM techniques (e.g., AMOS, Lisrel) when small sample sizes are used (Chin, 1998). Therefore, PLS is particularly beneficial when medium and complex models are estimated using small samples, as it is the case in this study.

Following PLS guidelines (Chin, 2010), the analysis was conducted in two stages. First, the relations between latent variables and observed indicators were examined for the measurement model. At this stage, reliability, convergent and discriminant validity of the latent constructs were evaluated. Secondly, the predictive relations among latent variables were examined in the structural model. Path coefficients and variance explained by the model were estimated.

Measurement model. The PLS path analysis showed that two indicator variables for the latent construct of social problems had outer loadings of less than .40, indicating that they should be dropped from the model (Hulland, 1999). These two indicators were "dependency" from the STRS scale and "asocial with peers" from the CBS scale. All other observed indicators showed acceptable to good outer loadings on their respective latent constructs (see Table 2).

Table 2
Measurement Model Evaluation Results

Constructs/Indicators	Source	Loading	Composite Reliability	AVE
Emotional Availability	EA		.92	.68
Mother sensitivity		.93		
Mother structuring		.84		
Mother nonintrusiveness		.48		
Mother nonhostility		.79		
Child involvement		.90		
Child responsiveness		.92		
Language Ability			.90	.82
Expressive score	EOWPVT	.90		
Receptive score	ROWPVT	.91		
Narratives	MSSB		.82	.61
Engagement and attention		.66		
Cognitive complexity		.89		
Affect tone		.78		

Table 2 Continued
Measurement Model Evaluation Results

	Source	Loading	Composite Reliability	AVE
T1 Social Competence			.92	.56
Prosocial with peers	CBS	.75		
Closeness	STRS	.45		
Frustration tolerance	TCRS	.75		
Assertive social skills	TCRS	.76		
Task Orientation	TCRS	.80		
Peer social skills	TCRS	.83		
Cooperation	SSRS	.78		
Assertion	SSRS	.69		
Self-Control	SSRS	.85		
T1 Social Problems			.90	.53
Aggressive with peers	CBS	.71		
Excluded by peers	CBS	.73		
Anxious-Fearful	CBS	.61		
Hyperactive-Distractible	CBS	.78		
Conflict	STRS	.70		
Acting out	TCRS	.81		
Shy/Anxious	TCRS	.63		
Learning Problems	TCRS	.83		
T2 Social Competence			.92	.55
Prosocial with peers	CBS	.68		
Closeness	STRS	.72		
Frustration tolerance	TCRS	.65		
Assertive social skills	TCRS	.76		
Task Orientation	TCRS	.81		
Peer social skills	TCRS	.84		
Cooperation	SSRS	.77		
Assertion	SSRS	.72		
Self-Control	SSRS	.71		
T2 Social Problems			.92	.58
Aggressive with peers	CBS	.78		
Excluded by peers	CBS	.77		
Anxious-Fearful	CBS	.54		
Hyperactive-Distractible	CBS	.85		
Conflict	STRS	.80		
Acting out	TCRS	.84		
Shy/anxious	TCRS	.71		
Learning problems	TCRS	.76		

In addition, latent constructs in the measurement model showed composite reliability values of .82 or higher, supporting the internal consistency of the measured constructs. Similarly, all average variance extracted (AVE) values are higher than the critical threshold value of .50, indicating good convergent validity of the measurement model.

Discriminant validity of the measurement model was examined by comparing the value of bivariate correlations among the latent constructs to the square root of the AVEs for each latent construct (see results in Table 3). The values of the square root of AVEs were greater than the bivariate correlations with all the other latent variables for emotional availability, language ability, and narratives indicating good discriminant validity of these three constructs. The exceptions are greater bivariate correlations among T1 social competence, T1 social problems, T2 social competence, and T2 social problems than the square root of each construct's AVE. However, the lack of discriminant validity among these four constructs is both reasonable and expected as they represent children's socioemotional developmental outcomes in kindergarten from either a strength-based or problem-based focus at two time points (one semester apart). Children's social competence and social problems showed strong negative associations at both time points and overtime, providing support for their construct validity. The strong positive associations between

Table 3
Correlations Among Constructs and the Square Root of AVEs of the Latent Constructs in the Measurement Model

	1	2	3	4	5	6	7
1. Emotional availability	**.82**						
2. Language ability	.24	**.91**					
3. Narratives	.27*	.40**	**.78**				
4. T1 social competence	.33*	.47***	.33*	**.75**			
5. T1 social problems	-.45***	-.40**	-.32*	-.79***	**.70**		
6. T2 social competence	.30*	.42**	.42**	.87***	-.75***	**.74**	
7. T2 social problems	-.39**	-.36**	-.31*	-.64***	.88***	-.70***	**.72**

Note. Values on the diagonal represent the square root of the AVE of each latent construct.
*$p < .05$; **$p < .01$; ***$p < .001$

T1 and T2 social competence, as well as between T1 and T2 social problems, suggested both test-retest reliability and developmental stability of these constructs. Taken together, these findings suggest that the measurement model had acceptable internal consistency, convergent validity, and discriminant validity.

Structural model. Path coefficients among the latent constructs and explained variances of the endogenous constructs were estimated using SmartPLS (Ringle et al., 2015). Bootstrapping procedures with 2000 subsamples were used to assess the significance of the path coefficients. The final PLS model is presented in Figure 2. Consistent with our hypotheses, prekindergarten EA was negatively associated with children's social problems, and quality of prekindergarten narratives was positively associated with children's social competence at the early stages of kindergarten adjustment. Furthermore, better language ability was associated with better quality of children's narratives. The intra-individual stability in social competence and social problems between the early stages and the later stages of kindergarten adjustment was strong. The associations between narratives and children's social competence at the later stages of kindergarten and children's social problems at the early stages of kindergarten were in the expected direction, but only reached a marginal level of statistical significance. Contrary to expectations, neither a significant association between EA and narratives, or the mediating effects of narratives between EA and

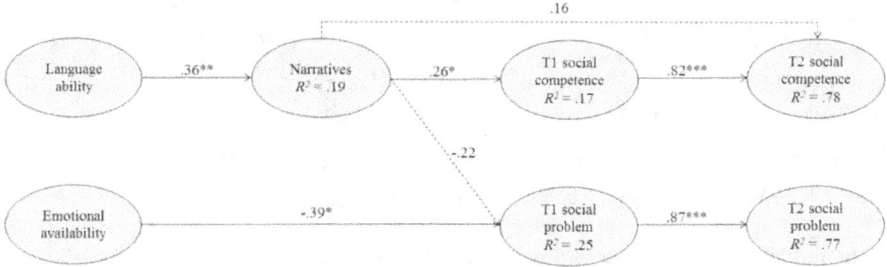

Figure 2. Path diagram showing relationships among the latent constructs.
Note. Non-significant paths were estimated but not displayed in the path diagram, except for two marginally significant paths from Narratives to T1 social problem and T2 social competence.
* $p < .05$; ** $p < .01$; *** $p < .001$

developmental outcomes were found.¹ Likely due to the strong stability of social competence and social problems over time, only earlier competence was found to be the significant predictor of later competence and only earlier problems was found to be the significant predictor of later problems.

In sum, the findings indicated that, for this sample, there may be different pathways for the development of social competence and social problems. The quality of earlier narratives was positively associated with children's language ability and social competence at the early stages of kindergarten adjustment, and social competence at the early stages was the strongest predictor of children's social competence at the later stages of kindergarten adjustment. Further, higher levels of prekindergarten parent-child EA were found to be predictive of fewer child social problems at the early stages of kindergarten adjustment, which further predicted lower levels of social problems at the later stages of kindergarten adjustment.

Discussion

We predicted that an overall latent construct of parent-child EA prior to kindergarten entry would predict children's social competence and social problems at both stages of kindergarten adjustment. This hypothesis was partly supported; mother-child EA during the prekindergarten year was negatively associated with child social problems during the kindergarten transition, but it was not significantly related to social competence at either time point. Findings relating EA and social problems are consistent with previous studies (Biringen et al., 2005; Kang, 2005) that also found that greater mother-child EA predicts fewer internalizing and externalizing behaviors. Our findings add to the prior literature in that EA prior to elementary school predicts child problems after school entry.

---

1. The model was also tested with individual EA dimensions as unique mediators of this relationship, as these dimensions more directly assess attachment-related behaviors. However, these models also did not reflect a mediating effect, and they otherwise did not substantially differ from the model using EA as a composite measure.

However, contrary to these findings using the EA latent construct, previous studies using individual EA dimensions have found relations between EA and social competence (Howes & Hong, 2008; Saunders, Sarche, Trucksess, Morse, & Biringen (2018). For example, Howes and Hong (2008) found that maternal sensitivity and structuring predicted young children's social competence, and Saunders et al. (2018) found significant relations between maternal structuring and child social-emotional competence. In this study also, the "smaller" analyses (zero-order correlations) between the EA dimensions and social competence showed meaningful relations suggesting that future studies should continue to examine EA dimensions individually in order to identify unique pathways to social adjustment, as well as to develop targeted interventions for families in order to prevent such problems.[2]

This study, among others (e.g., Biringen et al., 2005; Kang, 2005), demonstrates that the emotional quality of parent-child interactions predicts social outcomes that are relevant to school readiness and academic success. Children who experience emotionally available relationships with their mothers are less likely to demonstrate social problems, such as aggression, anxiety, and hyperactivity that could hinder their academic success. This conclusion is consistent with other studies demonstrating the importance of children's early relationships to their success in school and in social contexts (Brooks-Gunn & Marksman, 2005; Clark & Ladd, 2000; Commodore, 2012). Given that mother-child EA was assessed prior to school entry, interventions to improve EA can occur prior to kindergarten, specifically in families where this is seen as low.

We add to the above literature by testing whether the quality of children's narratives also predict children's social adjustment and

---

2. In the current study, the individual EA dimensions showed similar associations with the social competence and social problem constructs as did the latent EA construct. However, the current sample size was too small to provide a reasonable variable-participant ratio to include all individual EA dimensions and the outcome variables in a parsimonious model. Therefore, we chose to present results for the current model, which modeled EA as one latent construct with all individual EA dimensions as manifest variables.

mediate the relationships between EA and children's social competence and social problems at both stages of kindergarten adjustment. The current findings indicated that children's narratives directly predicted social competence. This study, among others (e.g., Shields et al., 2001; Stadelmann, Perren, von Wyl, & von Klitzing, 2007), indicates children who tell more coherent, creative, and emotionally rich stories, representing more positive internal working models are also more likely to demonstrate social competence including prosocial behavior, self-control, and peer social skills at least as reported by teachers. However, both mother-child EA and children's narrative quality showed direct relations with children's social relationships in kindergarten, but narratives did not have a mediational role.

Our final hypothesis predicted that children's social problems and social competence would demonstrate stability between the early adjustment and late adjustment phases of kindergarten. Both constructs demonstrated high stability across the school year supporting our hypothesis. Given the relevance of children's social skills to their academic and social success (Hamre & Pianta, 2001; Zins & Elias, 2006), these findings demonstrate the importance of intervening to address social problems so that they do not persist into later grades.

Consistent with prior research, language was a significant predictor of children's narratives and played a potentially confounding role. This suggests that linguistic ability (and particularly expressive language) is relevant to the quality of narratives that children tell. Therefore, future studies that examine children's narratives in relation to their social worlds should also examine language ability as a potential confounding variable. However, it is also important to note that children's verbal abilities are often strongly influenced by their social environments. For example, children raised in low-income families are exposed to significantly fewer words than their middle or upper-class counterparts, contributing to the ubiquitous "word gap" between social classes (Hart & Risley, 2003). Further, children exposed to interpersonal violence or other forms of trauma demonstrate delays in verbal ability (Graham-Bermann, Howell, Miller, Kwek, & Lilly, 2010). Therefore, children's social experiences, language abilities, narratives, and social outcomes are all likely intertwined and reciprocal. Future research should continue to use multiple time points and measurement tools in order to further examine these constructs.

Clinical Implications

The results of this study highlight the importance of intervening early, both in school settings and with parents, in order to promote young children's social-emotional well-being. Both social-emotional competence and social-emotional problems were highly stable across the kindergarten year. In other words, children who were socially adept during the first month of kindergarten were likely to remain adept at the end of the year, and children struggling socially at the beginning of the year were likely to still be experiencing challenges at the end of kindergarten. Programs that target social and emotional learning in school settings have been demonstrated to have positive impacts on children's academic achievement (Durlak, Weissberg, Dymnicki, Taylor, & Schellinger, 2011). Moreover, the promotion of social skills would ideally occur even before children enter kindergarten in order to prevent social and academic delays (Mashburn et al., 2008).

The findings of this study suggest that a 15-20 minute EA context in the prekindergarten year can predict children's adjustment, suggesting opportunities for parent-child coaching as part of preparing children for school. Helping parents learn to structure interactions may be an important tool in helping children curb their aggressive impulses and to enjoy more successful peer relationships. Therefore, it may be important to implement and evaluate interventions that prevent social problems among young children especially through their relationships with caregivers (Biringen et al., 2010; Biringen et al., 2015; Brooks-Gunn & Marksman, 2005; Early et al., 2007). Similarly, if children can be encouraged to tell stories in a complex, engaged, and positive manner, this, too may be a prevention goal.

Limitations and Conclusions

Some characteristics of this study limit its generalizability. First, the sample size was only 57 participants, and a larger sample size may produce more accurate estimation of standard errors. However, the statistical method used, PLS, is well-suited for modeling complex pathways among latent variables with smaller sample sizes. Furthermore, although the participants in this study were mainly Caucasian, the sample was fairly diverse by income with almost half of participants reporting an annual family income above $50,000 and half of mothers reporting less than a college education. Next, there were limitations to measurement methods. The same teachers reported on children's social problems and competence at both Time 1 and Time 2. This may explain the high degree of stability over time for teachers may have responded with bias based on their prior responses or history of experience with the student. Thus, future studies would benefit from using multiple informants or observational methods.

This study also had several notable strengths. First, it used both self-report and observational methods. The MSSB and the EAS both used observation or evaluation by trained researchers and both involved extensive training and reliability work. Social science researchers have warned about problems associated with relying entirely on self-report measures, for participants are often likely to respond with social desirability bias (Cook & Campbell, 1979). Thus, using both observational and self-report methods may have reduced the bias that can accompany self-report measures.

In closing, scholars have long theorized about the ways in which children's social experiences get internalized and, subsequently, projected onto new relationships (Bowlby, 1980; Bretherton, 1990). This study helps to paint part of the picture demonstrating the ways in which the emotional quality of parent-child interactions predict children's social problems, as well as how children's quality of stories predict positive social interactions with peers. Further, our results demonstrate the stability of social competence and social problems during the first year of formal school, highlighting the need for early intervention or coaching on mother-child EA and/or children's ability to tell stories. Future research should continue to examine how social experiences get "under the skin" and how to best promote young children's positive social development especially as they embark on one of their hardest challenges yet, kindergarten.

Author's Note
Study procedures were approved by Colorado State University Institutional Review Board. Funding from the National Science Foundation, grant number 9973396, was awarded to Dr. Biringen. Dr. Biringen reports a conflict of interest, as the EA Scales were developed by her, but she reports no financial conflict of interest with the participants of this study.

References

Birch, S. H., & Ladd, G. W. (1997). The teacher-child relationship and children's early school adjustment. *Journal of School Psychology, 35*, 61–79. doi:10.1016/S0022-4405(96)00029-5

Biringen, Z. (2008). *The Emotional Availability (EA) Scales and the Emotional Attachment & Emotional Availability (EA2) Clinical Screener (4th ed.): Infancy/Early Childhood Version; Middle Childhood/Youth Versions; Therapist/Interventionist Manual; Couple Relationship Manual.* Boulder, CO. Retrieved from http://emotionalavailabilty.com.

Biringen, Z., Batten, R., Neelan, P., Altenhofen, S., Swaim, R., Bruce, A., Fetsch, R., Voitel, C., & Zachary, V. (2010). Emotional availability (EA): The assessment of and intervention for global parent-child relational quality. *Journal of Experiential Psychotherapy, 49*, 3–9.

Biringen, Z., Closson, L., Derr-Moore, A., Warren, V., Lucas-Thompson, R., Harman, J., & Neu, M. (2015). Mindfulness, emotional availability, and emotional attachment: Three pillars of daily practice. *Zero to Three Journal*, 20–26.

Biringen, Z., Damon, J., Grigg, W., Mone, J., Pipp-Seigal, S., Skillern, S., & Stratton, J. (2005). Emotional availability: Differential predictions to infant attachment and kindergarten adjustment based on observation time and context. *Infant Mental Health Journal, 26*(4), 295–308.

Biringen, Z., Derscheid, D., Vliegen, N., Closson, L., & Easterbrooks, A.E. (2014). Emotional availability (EA): Theoretical background, empirical research using the EA Scales, and clinical applications. *Developmental Review, 34*, 93–188.

Biringen, Z., & Easterbrooks, M. A. (2012). Emotional availability: Concept, research, and window on developmental psychopathology. *Development and psychopathology, 24*(1), 1-8. doi: 10.1017/s0954579411000617

Biringen, Z., Robinson, J., & Emde, R. (1998). *Emotional Availability Scales, 3rd Edition.* Unpublished Manual for the EAS-training. Retrieved from www.emotionalavailability.com

Bowlby, J. (1969). *Attachment and loss* (Vol. 1). New York, NY: Basic Books.

Bowlby, J. (1980). *Attachment and loss* (Vol. 2). New York, NY: Basic Books.

Bretherton, I. (1990). Communication patterns, internal working models, and the intergenerational transmission of attachment relationships. *Infant Mental Health Journal, 11*(3), 237-252.

Bretherton, I., Oppenheim, D., Emde, R. N., & the MacArthur Narrative Working Group (2003). The MacArthur Story Stem Battery. In R. N. Emde, D. P. Wolf, & D. Oppenheim (Eds.), *Revealing the inner worlds of young children: The MacArthur Story Stem Battery and parent-child narratives* (pp. 381-396). New York, NY: Oxford University Press.

Brooks-Gunn, J. & Markman, L.B. (2005). The contribution of parenting to ethnic and racial gaps in school readiness. *Future of Children, 15*, 139-168.

Brownell, R. (2000). *Receptive and Expressive One-Word Picture Vocabulary Tests.* New York, NY: PsychCorp.

Chin, W. W. (1998). The partial least squares approach for structural equation modeling. In G. A. Marcoulides (Ed.), *Modern methods for business research* (pp. 295-336). Hillsdale, NJ: Lawrence Erlbaum Associates.

Chin, W. W. (2010). How to write up and report PLS analyses. In V.E. Vinzi, W.W. Chin, J. Henseler, H. Wang (Eds.). *Handbook of partial least squares: Concepts, methods and applications* (pp. 655-690). New York, NY: Springer.

Clark, K. E., & Ladd, G. W. (2000). Connectedness and autonomy support in parent-child relationships: Links to children's socioemotional orientation and peer relations. *Developmental Psychology, 36*, 485-498. doi:10.1037//0012-1649.36.4.485

Commodari, E. (2013). Preschool teacher attachment, school readiness and risk of learning difficulties. *Early Childhood Research Quarterly, 28*, 123-133. doi:10.1016/j.ecresq.2012.03.004

Cook, T. D., & Campbell, D. T. (1979). *Quasi-experimentation: Design and analysis issues.* Boston, MA: Houghton Mifflin.

Durlak, J. A., Weissberg, R. P., Dymnicki, A. B., Taylor, R. D., & Schellinger, K. B. (2011). The impact of enhancing students' social and emotional learning: A meta-analysis of school-based universal interventions. *Child Development, 82,* 405–432. doi:10.1111/j.1467-8624.2010.01564.x

Dykas, M. J., & Cassidy, J. (2011). Attachment and the processing of social information across the life span: Theory and evidence. *Psychological Bulletin, 137,* 19–46. doi:10.1037/a0021367

Early, D. M., Maxwell, K. L., Buchinall, M., Alva, S., Bender, R. H., Bryant, D., & Zill, N. (2007). Teachers' education, classroom quality, and young children's academic skills: Results from seven studies of preschool programs. *Child Development, 78,* 558–580. doi:0009-3920/2007/7802-0013.

Fiorentino, L., & Howe, N. (2004). Language competence, narrative ability, and school readiness in low-income preschool children. *Canadian Journal of Behavioural Science, 36*(4), 280–294.

Fornell, C., & Bookstein, F. L. (1982). Two structural equation models: LISREL and PLS applied to consumer exit-voice theory. *Journal of Marketing Research, 19,* 440–452.

Frank, F. R., & Miller, N. B. (1992). *A primer for soft modeling.* Akron, OH: University of Akron Press.

George, C., Kaplan, N., & Main, M. (1984). *The Adult Attachment Interview.* Unpublished protocol, University of California at Berkeley.

Graham-Bermann, S. A., Howell, K. H., Miller, L. E., Kwek, J., & Lilly, M. M. (2010). Traumatic events and maternal education as predictors of verbal ability for preschool children exposed to intimate partner violence (IPV). *Journal of Family Violence, 25*(4), 383–392. doi:10.1007/s10896-009-9299-3

Gralinki, H. J., & Kopp, C. B. (1993). Everyday rules for behavior: Mothers' requests to young children. *Developmental Psychology, 29,* 573–584.

Gresham, F. M., & Elliot, S. N. (1990). Social skills rating system manual. Circle Pines, MN: American Guidance Service.

Hamre, B. K., & Pianta, R. C. (2001). Early teacher-child relationships and the trajectory of children's school outcomes through eighth grade. *Child Development, 72,* 625–638. doi:10.1111/1467-8624.00301

Hart, B., & Risley, T. R. (2003). The early catastrophe: The 30 million word gap by age 3. *American Educator, 27*(1), 4–9.

Hightower, A. D., Work, W. C., Cowen, E. L., Lotyczewski, B. S., Spinell, A. P., Guare, J. C., & Rohrbeck, C. A. (1986). The teacher-child rating scale: A brief objective measure of elementary children's school problem behaviors and competencies. *School Psychology Review, 15*(3), 393–409.

Howes, C., & Hong, S. S. (2008). Early emotional availability: Predictive of pre-kindergarten relationships among Mexican heritage children? *Journal of Early Childhood and Infant Psychology, 4*, 4–26.

Howes, C., Phillipsen, L. C., & Peisner-Feinberg, E. (2000). Consistency of perceived teacher-child relationships between preschool and kindergarten. *Journal of School Psychology, 38*, 113–132. doi:10.1016/S0022-4405(99)00044-8

Hulland, J. (1999). Use of partial least squares (PLS) in strategic management research: A review of four recent studies. *Strategic Management Journal, 20*, 195–204.

Justice, L. M., Bowles, R. P., Pence Turnbull, K. L., & Skibbe, L. E. (2009). School readiness among children with varying histories of language difficulties. *Developmental Psychology, 45*, 460–476. doi:10.1037/a0014324

Kang, M. J. (2005). *Quality of mother-child interaction assessed by the emotional availability scale: Associations with maternal psychological well-being, child behavior problems and child cognitive functioning* (Order No. 3182762). Available from ProQuest Dissertations & Theses Global. (305430591). Retrieved from http://ezproxy.library.tamu.edu/login?url=https://search.proquest.com/docview/305430591?accountid=7082

Ladd, G. W., & Profilet, S. M. (1996). The Child Behavior Scale: A teacher-report measure of young children's aggressive, withdrawn, and prosocial behaviors. *Developmental Psychology, 32*, 1008–1024.

Laible, D., Carlo, G., Torquati, J., & Ontai, L. (2004). Children's perceptions of family relationships as assessed in a doll story completion task: Links to parenting, social competence, and externalizing behavior. *Social Development, 13*, 551–569.

Mashburn, A. J., Pianta, R. C., Hamre, B. K., Towner, J. T., Barbarin, O. A., Bryant, D., … Howes, C. (2008). Measures of classroom quality in prekindergarten and children's development of academic, language, and social skills. *Child Development, 79*, 732–749. doi:0009-3920/208/7903-0016.

McCabe, P. C., & Meller, P. J. (2004) The relationship between language and social competence: Language impairment affects social growth. *Psychology in the Schools, 41*, 313–321. doi:10.1002/pits.10161

Murray, C., & Murray, K. M. (2004). Child level correlates of student-teacher relationships: An examination of demographic characteristics, academic orientations, and behavioural orientations. *Psychology in the Schools, 41*, 751–762. doi:10.1002/pits.20015

Pianta, R. C. (2001). *The Student Teacher Relationship Scale.* Lutz, FL: Psychological Assessment Resources.

Rimm-Kaufman, S. E., & Pianta, R. C. (2000). An ecological perspective on the transition to kindergarten: A theoretical framework to guide empirical research. *Journal of Applied Developmental Psychology, 21*, 491–511.

Ringle, C. M., Wende, S., & Becker, J. M. (2015). *SmartPLS 3*. Boenningstedt, Germany: SmartPLS GmbH.

Rudasill, K. M., & Rimm-Kaufmann, S. E. (2009). Teacher-child relationship quality: The roles of child temperament and teacher-child interactions. *Early Childhood Research Quarterly, 24*, 107–120. doi:10.1016/j.ecresq.2008.12.003

Saunders, H., Sarche, M., Trucksess, C., Morse, B., & Biringen, Z. (2018). Parents' adverse childhood experiences and parent-child emotional availability in an American Indian community: Relations with young children's social-emotional development. Manuscript submitted for publication.

Shields, A., Ryan, R. M., & Cicchetti, D. (2001). Narrative representations of caregivers and emotion dysregulation predictors of maltreated children's rejection by peers. *Developmental Psychology, 37*, 321–337.

Solomonica-Levi, D., Yirmiya, N., Erel, O., Samet, I., & Oppenheim, D. (2001). The associations among observed maternal behavior, children's narrative representations of mothers, and children's behavior problems. *Journal of Social and Personal Relationships, 18*, 673–690.

Sroufe, L. A. (2000). Early relationships and the development of children. *Infant Mental Health Journal, 21*, 67–74.

Stadelmann, S., Perren, S., von Wyl, A., & von Klitzing, K. (2007). Associations between family relationships and symptoms/strengths at kindergarten age: What is the role of children's parental representations? *Journal of Child Psychology and Psychiatry, 48*, 996–1004.

Trickett, P. K., McBride-Chang, C., & Putman, F. W. (1994). The classroom performance and behavior of sexually abused females. *Development and Psychopathology, 6*, 183–194.

Van der Oord, S., Van der Meulen, E. M., Prins, P. J. M., Oosterlaan, J., Buitelaar, J. K., & Emmelkamp, P. M. G. (2005). A psychometric evaluation of the social skills rating system in children with attention deficit hyperactivity disorder. *Behaviour Research and Therapy, 43*, 733–746.

Whiting, B. B., & Edwards, C. P. (1988). *Children of different worlds: The formation of social behavior*. Cambridge, MA: Harvard University Press.

Zins, J. E., & Elias, M. J. (2006). Social and emotional learning. In G. G. Bear & K. M. Minke (Eds.), *Children's needs III: Development, prevention, and intervention* (pp. 1–13). Bethesda, MD: National Association of School Psychologists.

Concurrent and Predictive Relationships Between the Bayley-III and Stanford-Binet 5

Laura E. Murphy, Colby D. Taylor, and Randy G. Floyd

Abstract

The Bayley Scales of Infant Development-III (Bayley-III) were compared to the concurrently administered Stanford-Binet Intelligence Scales, Fifth Edition (SB5) for 80 children ages 27–42 months: 38 with autism spectrum disorder, 11 with global developmental delay, 6 with attention-deficit/hyperactivity disorder, and 25 children with no diagnosis. A composite score for the Bayley-III was developed by averaging the Language and Cognitive Scales of the Bayley-III, and all scores were contrasted with the Verbal, Nonverbal, Full Scale IQ, and Abbreviated IQ of the SB5 and five SB5 factor scores. Children generally scored significantly higher on the Bayley-III than on the SB5 for all groups, including the comparison group of children with no known disability. However, Bayley-III and SB5 scores were strongly correlated for all children. Bayley-III scores were also moderately to highly correlated with SB5 scores administered to 35 children months later. With the exception of some factor comparisons, SB5 scores for 40 children were highly correlated with SB5 scores administered months later.

Keywords: preschool assessment, intellectual functioning, infant and toddler development

Assessment of preschool children presents challenges that may not manifest as frequently in assessment of individuals who are older. Preschoolers may have less emotional regulation, and their behavior may vary considerably from day to day (Nagle, 2000). They may have low frustration tolerance, limited concentration and attention, as well as significant distractibility. Preschoolers' receptive language may be limited, and they may tire easily. Further, within days or months, preschool children may experience growth spurts resulting in fluctuations in test performance (Bracken, 1987; Bracken & Nagle, 2007; Bracken & Walker, 1997; Brassard & Boehm, 2007). Although assessing young children can be challenging, federal legislation mandates the early identification of preschoolers with developmental delays, thereby necessitating the careful selection of the most reliable and valid instruments available for this age range.

Norm referenced tests (NRT) are useful tools in the identification of preschool developmental concerns. NRT may be used to assess baseline functioning for a preschool child entering early intervention (Brassard & Boehm, 2007) and to determine current functioning compared to a nationally representative sample of individuals of comparable age or to a special group of individuals with global developmental delays (GDD), autism spectrum disorder (ASD), attention deficit hyperactivity disorder (ADHD), or other developmental disabilities. Although the psychometrics of preschool NRT have steadily improved over the last few decades (Nagle, 2017), not all preschool assessment instruments are supported by extensive and representative norming, adequate item scaling, and sound reliability and validity evidence. Recent norming, strong internal consistency (.90), high test-retest stability (.90), adequate test floors (spanning two or more standard deviations below the mean), and relatively evenly-spaced item gradients are especially important for preschool assessment instruments (Bracken, 1987; Bradley-Johnson & Durmusoglu, 2005; Brassard & Boehm, 2007). Two instruments, the Bayley Scales of Infant Development-III (Bayley-III; Bayley, 2005, 2006a, 2006b) and the Stanford-Binet Intelligence Scales, Fifth Edition (SB5;

Roid, 2003a, 2003b, 2003c) are among the most common instruments used to identify preschool developmental delay (Camara, Nathan, & Puente, 2000; Johnson, Moore, & Marlow, 2014; Scattone, Raggio, & May, 2011). Both appeal to young children by including toys in the test materials and varying activities during the assessment.

According to Sattler (2008), the "Bayley-III is the best available instrument for the assessment of infants. The norm group was excellent and the technical properties are good" (p. 678). Vig and Sanders (2007) conveyed, "Due to its strong psychometric and clinical properties, the Bayley-III is the best choice for assessing children up to 42 months of age" (p. 396). The Bayley-III is often referred to as the "gold standard" assessment of infant and toddler development (Johnson et al., 2014; Rubio-Codina, Araujo, Attanasio, Munoz, & Grantham-McGregor, 2016; Scattone et al., 2011). The Bayley-III has some psychometric properties that are better than many preschool instruments. It has relatively narrow age spans per norm block (1–3 months), resulting in very little change in scores with slight age gain for the child, which is a desirable characteristic in preschool assessment. Bayley-III item gradients and floors are adequate, and these are strengths compared to most preschool instruments (Bradley-Johnson & Johnson, 2007). In addition, the Bayley-III boasts strong internal consistencies for ages 24–42 months (.92 to .97 for Cognitive, .93 to .96 for Receptive Communication, .96 to .97 for Expressive Communication; Bayley, 2006b).

With the most recent revision in 2005, the Bayley-III has been scrutinized. Infant testing has not been shown to strongly predict later intellectual functioning (Molfese & Acheson, 1997; Sternberg, Grigorenko, & Bundy, 2001; Weisglas-Kuperus, Baerts, & Sauer, 1993). Furthermore, with the recent revision, the Bayley-III authors did not present evidence supporting its validity over time. Thus, concerns about the predictive validity of the Bayley-III remain (Aylward, 2009; Bradley-Johnson & Johnson, 2007). Further, although the literature is somewhat mixed (Anderson & Burnett, 2017; Bos, 2013), many recent studies of preterm infants and at-risk preschoolers have found significantly higher scores on the Bayley-III than the Bayley-II (Acton et al., 2011; Anderson, Deluca, Hutchinson, Roberts, & Doyle, 2010; Jary, Whitelaw, Walloe, & Thoresen, 2013; Long, Galea, Eldridge, & Harris, 2012; Moore, Johnson, Haider, Hennessey, & Marlow, 2012; Silveira, Filipouski, Goldstein, O'Shea, & Procianoy, 2012; Vohr et al., 2012).

The standardization sample of the Bayley-III has also drawn criticism for possible over-representation of children with lower abilities. In a sample of children diagnosed with a developmental disability, the cognitive score of the Bayley-III only identified 22% of the children as having a developmental disability, while the language score only identified 47.5% of the children as having a developmental disability (Milne, McDonald, & Comino, 2012). Johnson et al. (2014) similarly found that the Bayley-III under-identifies children with developmental delay and suggest that practitioners consider using standard scores of 80 or 85, rather than 70, to more accurately identify children. However, there is some evidence that the Bayley-III can be used to distinguish between low-risk infants and infants at-risk for developmental delay (Yu et al., 2013). In examining predictive validity, the Bayley-III may be a good predictor of future intelligence for disabled populations, but not for children of average intellectual ability (Chinta, Walker, Halliday, Loughran-Fowlds, & Badawi, 2014). This criticism is not specific to the Bayley-III, as a concern of infant intelligence tests is that they do not predict future cognitive functioning (Neisser et al., 1996). Despite concerns about discriminability and predictability, the Bayley-III is still one of the most psychometrically sound tests of its kind (Geisinger, Spies, Carlson, & Plake, 2007; Kaplan & Saccuzzo, 2017).

The Stanford-Binet Intelligence Scales, Fifth Edition (SB5) is another commonly used instrument for preschool testing. As the oldest standardized measure of intellectual functioning, the SB5 has led to more research publications than any other instrument (Becker, 2003). The SB5 and its predecessors have been among the 20 most commonly administered tests by psychologists in the United States since 1935, and the test remains one of the three most commonly administered cognitive assessments (Camara et al., 2000). The most recent revision has excellent internal consistency for its Full Scale IQ (.97 for all ages and .98 for children ages 2–3 years), Nonverbal IQ (.95 and .96, respectively), and Verbal IQ (.95 and .96, respectively). The SB5 factor scores also have strong internal consistency coefficients, ranging from .86 for Fluid Reasoning to .95 for Knowledge for children ages 2–3 years. Like the Bayley-III, the SB5 also has relatively narrow norm blocks (2 months). A review by Alfonso and Flanagan (2007) stated that the SB5 has "better floors than those comprising other intelligence batteries with norms for preschoolers" (p. 279). The SB5 measures cognitive functioning for children as young as 24 months. However, for children ages 24–42 months, the SB5 floor may not finely differentiate ability levels among preschoolers, as no children younger than 42 months with intellectual disabilities were included in the norm group (Finello, 2011). Additionally, although the SB5 has adequate item gradients for most subtests at 60 months, the item gradients are not adequate to differentiate subtest skills for ages 24–30 months (Alfonso & Flanagan, 2007).

As there are a limited number of assessment instruments appropriate for preschoolers, few studies have concurrently examined the Bayley-III and other measures of cognition. Recently, Kamppi and Gilmore (2010) examined the relations between Bayley-III and SB5 scores in a concurrent validity study. With the exception of the SB5 Knowledge factor and the Bayley-III Language score ($r = .41$), they did not find statistically significant associations (-.18 to .35) between cross-battery scores. However, Kamppi and Gilmore assessed a small sample of 26 typically developing children who displayed little variance in scores. Although the predictive validity of the Bayley-III has been examined by Bode, D'Eugenio, Mettelman, and Gros (2014) and Spencer-Smith, Spittle, Lee, Doyle, and Anderson (2015) in relation to the Wechsler Preschool and Primary Scale of Intelligence, Third Edition (WPPSI - III; Wechsler, 2002), and Differential Ability Scales, Second Edition (Elliott, 2007), the predictive validity of the Bayley-III has not, to date, been analyzed in relation to the SB5. To expand on the limited information in this area, we sought to examine the concurrent and predictive validity of the Bayley-III and SB5 for both typically developing children as well as for children with developmental delays who were evaluated at a center for developmental disabilities.

The following 10 hypotheses were made:
- Bayley-III Full Scale Average (FSA),[1] Cognitive, and Language will yield significantly higher scores than the SB5 Full Scale IQ (FSIQ), Nonverbal IQ (NVIQ), and Verbal IQ (VIQ).
- Bayley-III FSA will strongly correlate with SB5 FSIQ and Abbreviated IQ.
- Bayley-III Language Composite (as well as Receptive Communication and Expressive Communication) will strongly correlate with the SB5 VIQ.
- Bayley-III Cognitive Composite will strongly correlate with the SB5 NVIQ.
- Bayley-III FSA will correlate most strongly with the SB5 Knowledge and Working Memory factors.
- Bayley-III and SB5 correlations will be stronger in representing concurrent relationships than predictive relationships.
- Bayley-III and SB5 will yield statistically higher scores for the Comparison group than the Clinical group of children with known developmental disabilities.
- Bayley-III and SB5 scores will strongly correlate with one another when analyzed independently for both the Clinical group and the Comparison group of children with no known disabilities.
- Initial SB5 (1.SB5) and follow-up SB5 (2.SB5) scores will strongly correlate with one another when analyzed independently for both the Clinical group and the Comparison group of children with no known developmental disability.

---

1. Based on Moore et al. (2012) and Johnson et al. (2014), we averaged the Bayley-III cognitive and language composites and labeled it the Bayley-III Full Scale Average (Bayley-III FSA).

- Initial SB5 (1.SB5) and later (2.SB5) scores will yield significantly higher scores for the Comparison group than the Clinical group.

Method

Participants

Concurrent Sample. A total of 80 participants (64 boys, 16 girls) ranging from 27–42 months ($M = 35.38$, $SD = 5.53$) completed the Bayley-III and SB5 at initial testing. Licensed psychologists administered the tests or supervised the administration of testing by doctoral level graduate students in school or clinical psychology. The overall Concurrent Sample was composed of 43 African American or Black children, 27 European or White children, 4 Asian American children, 4 Hispanic American children, and 2 children in the Other Ethnic category as reported by caregiver. Parents of the 4 Hispanic American children reported that English and Spanish were spoken in the home, while parents of the 4 Asian American children reported that English and Chinese ($n = 1$) or only English ($n = 3$) were spoken in the home.

A Concurrent Clinical Sample of participants seeking a developmental disabilities evaluation from a developmental disabilities (DD) diagnostic center affiliated with the health science center of a large southern city was selected if participants were in the overlapping age range for the Bayley-III and SB5, ages 24–42 months. There were no efforts to limit the sample size of the Clinical Sample. Because evaluations for more boys than girls were sought at the DD center and because developmental disabilities are diagnosed at higher rates in boys than girls (American Psychiatric Association, 2013), there were more boys than girls in the samples. In addition, the majority of the children in the city where the health science center is located were African American. Therefore, compared to the United States population, there was an over representation of African Americans in the analyses.

The Concurrent Clinical Sample consisted of 55 children (45 boys, 10 girls). Participant ages ranged from 27–42 months ($M = 35.38$, $SD = 5.53$). The most frequent diagnosis in the Concurrent Clinical Sample was ASD (Concurrent $n = 38$). Most (69%) of the Concurrent Clinical Sample children with ASD also had dually diagnosed global developmental delay (GDD). Of the children in the Concurrent Clinical Sample without ASD, there were diagnoses of GDD ($n = 11$) and ADHD ($n = 6$).

A Concurrent Comparison Sample containing participants with no diagnoses was recruited from the daycare center for typically developing children of the same health science center. This sample included 25 children (19 boys, 6 girls) ranging in age from 27–41 months ($M = 35.88$, $SD = 4.03$). The Concurrent Comparison Sample numbers were limited by the small size of the daycare center. Moreover, to facilitate comparison with the Clinical Sample, more boys than girls were tested in the Comparison Sample.

Bayley-III/SB5 Predictive Sample (Predictive 1). A total of 35 participants (27 boys, 8 girls) ranging from 27–42 months ($M = 36.00$, $SD = 4.41$) completed the Bayley-III at initial testing and follow-up SB5 testing (2.SB5) at 41–65 months ($M = 52.89$, $SD = 6.01$). Licensed psychologists or supervised doctoral psychology students administered Predictive 1 and 2 testings. Most of the same psychologists had administered the SB5 and Bayley-III in the previous concurrent testing but were randomly assigned without attempts to have the same examiner test the same participant in both the concurrent and predictive test conditions. This sample was composed of 22 African American or Black children, 9 European or White children, and 4 Asian American children as reported by caregiver from the DD or university daycare center.

The Predictive 1 Clinical Sample consisted of 15 children (13 boys, 2 girls). Participant ages ranged from 28–42 months ($M = 36.27$, $SD = 5.52$) at initial Bayley-III. The age at follow-up SB5 testing ranged from 41–65 months ($M = 53.73$, $SD = 8.47$). This Predictive 1 Clinical Sample was composed of 8 African American or Black children,

5 European or White children, and 2 Asian American children as reported by caregiver. All were from the university DD center. The most frequent diagnosis in the Predictive 1 Clinical Sample was ASD ($n = 13$). Of the children in the Predictive Clinical Sample without ASD, there were diagnoses of GDD ($n = 1$) and ADHD ($n = 1$).

The Predictive 1 Comparison Sample consisted of 20 children (14 boys, 6 girls). Participant ages ranged from 27–41 months ($M = 35.80$, $SD = 3.45$) at initial Bayley-III testing. The age at follow-up SB5 testing ranged from 48–62 months ($M = 52.25$, $SD = 3.29$). This Predictive Comparison Sample was composed of 14 African American or Black children, 4 European or White children, and 2 Asian American children as reported by caregiver. All were from the university daycare center. There were no known diagnoses as reported by caregiver.

SB5/SB5 Predictive Sample (Predictive 2). A total of 40 participants (23 boys, 9 girls) ranging from 27–42 months ($M = 35.90$, $SD = 4.36$) completed the SB5 at initial testing (1.SB5) and follow-up SB5 testing (2.SB5) at 41–65 months ($M = 52.65$, $SD = 5.71$). This Sample was composed of 23 African American or Black children, 13 European or White children, and 4 Asian American children from the DD or university daycare center.

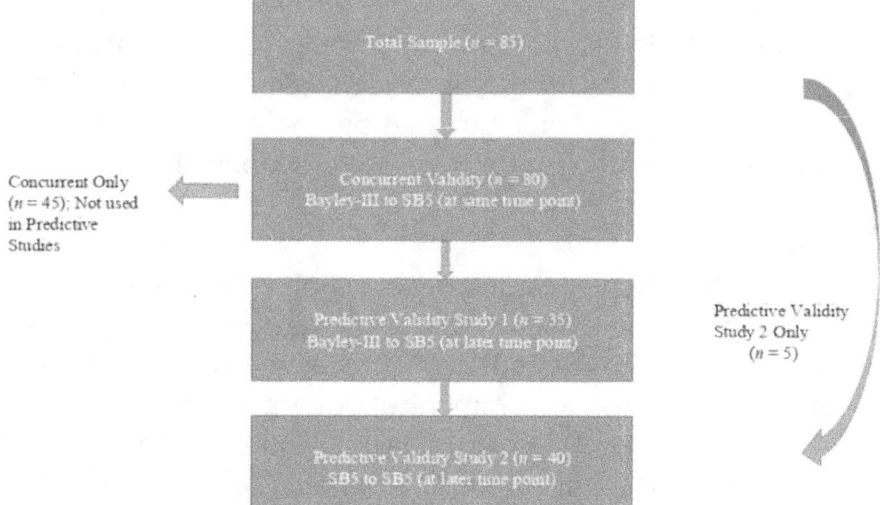

Figure 1. Participants in Bayley-III/Stanford Binet 5(SB5) Studies

The Predictive 2 Clinical Sample consisted of 18 children (16 boys, 2 girls). Participant ages ranged from 28–42 months ($M = 36.17$, $SD = 5.44$) at initial SB5 (1.SB5). The age at follow-up SB5 (2.SB5) testing ranged from 41–65 months ($M = 53.44$, $SD = 7.77$). This Predictive 2 Clinical Sample was composed of 9 African American or Black children, 7 European or White children, and 2 Asian American children. All were from the university DD center. The most frequent diagnosis in the Predictive 2 Clinical Sample was ASD ($n = 15$). Of the children in the Predictive Clinical Sample without ASD, there were diagnoses of GDD ($n = 2$) and ADHD ($n = 1$).

The Predictive 2 Comparison Sample consisted of 22 children (15 boys, 7 girls). Participant ages ranged from 27–41 months ($M = 35.68$, $SD = 3.34$) at initial SB5 testing (1.SB5). The age at follow-up SB5 (2.SB5) testing ranged from 48–62 months ($M = 52.00$, $SD = 3.27$). This Predictive 2 Comparison Sample was composed of 14 African American or Black children, 6 European or White children, and 2 Asian American children. All were from the university daycare center. There were no known diagnoses as reported by caregiver.

Although all of Predictive 1 Analysis were in Predictive 2 Analysis, 5 participants were not administered the Bayley-III and therefore were not participants in Predictive 1. With the addition of these 5 Predictive 2 children, the overall number of participants in the concurrent and predictive analyses was 85 (68 boys, 17 girls). Please refer to Figure 1 for further explanation and refer to Table 1 for demographic descriptions of all samples described above.

Measures

Cognitive. The Bayley-III (Bayley, 2006) is a norm-referenced test designed to individually assess children ages 16 days to 42 months. The Bayley-III is composed of five Scales: Cognitive, Language (Receptive and Expressive Communication), Motor (Fine and Gross), Social-Emotional, and Adaptive-Behavior. Only the Cognitive and Language Scales were utilized in the present study. The Cognitive Composite ($M = 100$, $SD = 15$) consists of items developed around

Table 1
Demographic Characteristics by Analyses

Bayley-III/SB5 Concurrent Analysis		
Concurrent Analysis, n = 80	Concurrent Clinical Sample, n = 55	Concurrent Comparison Sample, n = 25
64 males, 16 females	45 males, 10 females	19 males, 6 females
AA = 43, EA = 27, Asian = 4, Latino = 4, Other = 2	AA = 27, EA = 21. Asian = 2, Latino = 3, Other =2	AA = 16, EA = 6, Asian = 2, Latino = 1
Clinical Diagnosis = 55; No Diagnosis = 25	Autism Spectrum Disorder (ASD) = 38, Attention Deficit Hyperactivity Disorder (ADHD) = 6, Global Developmental Delay (GDD) = 11	No Diagnoses
Months of age M 35.38 (5.53), 27–42 month range	Months of age M = 35.38 (5.53), 27–42 months age range	Months of age M = 35.88 (4.03), 27–41 age range

Bayley-III/2.SB5 Predictive: Predictive 1 Analysis		
Predictive Analysis, n = 35	Predictive Clinical, n = 15	Predictive Comparison, n = 20
27 males, 8 females	13 males, 2 females	14 males, 16 females
AA = 22, EA = 9, Asian = 4	AA = 8, EA = 5, Asian = 2	AA = 14, EA = 4, Asian = 2
Clinical Diagnosis = 15; No Diagnosis = 20	ASD = 13, ADHD = 1, GDD = 1	No Diagnoses
1. Months of age M = 36.00 (4.41), 27–42 month range at initial testing 2. Months of age M = 52.89 (6.01), 41–65 month age range at follow-up	1. Months of age M = 36.27 (5.52), 28–42 month range at initial testing 2. Months of age M = 53.73 (8.47), 41–65 month age range at follow-up	1. Months of age M = 35.80 (3.45), 27–41 month range at initial testing 2. Months of age M = 52.25 (3.29), 48–62 month age range at follow-up

Table 1 Continued
Demographic Characteristics by Analyses

1.SB5/2.SB5: Predictive 2 Analysis		
Predictive Analysis, n = 40	Predictive Clinical, n = 18	Predictive Comparison, n = 22
31 males, 9 females	16 males, 2 females	15 males, 7 females
AA = 23, EA = 13, Asian = 4	AA = 9, EA = 7, Asian = 2	AA = 14, EA = 6, Asian = 2
Clinical Diagnosis = 18; No Diagnosis = 22	ASD = 15, ADHD = 1, GDD = 2	No Diagnoses
1. Months of age M = 35.90 (4.36), 27–42 month range at initial testing 2. Months of age M = 52.65 (5.71), 41–65 month age range at follow-up	1. Months of age M = 36.17 (5.44), 28–42 month range at initial testing 2. Months of age M = 53.44 (7.77), 41–65 month age range at follow-up	1. Months of age M = 35.68 (3.34), 27–41 month range at initial testing 2. Months of age M = 52.00 (3.27), 48–62 month age range at follow-up

visual attention and memory, speed of processing, discrimination of pictures, color recognition and matching, levels of play, and number constructs. The Language Composite (M = 100, SD = 15) is composed of two parts: receptive communication and expressive communication. Receptive communication assesses how well children understand spoken words and directions. Expressive communication assesses how well children communicate using words and gestures. Strong internal consistency has been demonstrated for children age 24–42 months, ranging from .92 to .97 for the Cognitive Scale and .93 to .97 for the Language Scale.

The SB5 (Roid, 2003) is a norm-referenced test designed for people age 2 to 85 years and more. The SB5 yields a VIQ (M = 100, SD = 15) and a NVIQ that are combined to produce a Full Scale IQ (FSIQ). Internal consistency is very strong, ranging from .95 to .98 for the VIQ, NVIQ, and FSIQ for ages 2–3 years. Each of five factors—Fluid Reasoning, Knowledge, Quantitative Reasoning, Visual Spatial Processing, and Working Memory—has a verbal and nonverbal subtest yielding a factor score ($M = 100$, $SD = 15$). Good to high internal consistency has been demonstrated for children age 2–3 years, ranging from the lowest (.86) for 2-year Fluid Reasoning to the highest (.95) for 2-year Knowledge. The SB5 also provides an Abbreviated IQ (ABIQ) composed of one nonverbal subtest, Fluid Reasoning, and the one verbal subtest, Knowledge. This ABIQ split-half reliability is .90 for 2-year-olds and .89 for 3-year-olds.

Procedure

Concurrent Validity: Concurrent Analyses 1. Assessed at a developmental disabilities center affiliated with a health science center in a large Southern city, 80 children completed the Bayley-III and SB5 in succession. Forty-five of the children completed the Bayley-III first, whereas 35 completed the SB5 first. Five children who were initially assigned to the SB5 had to be administered the Bayley-III first due to physician referral. The Bayley-III and SB5 were completed on the same day for 76 children. Four children completed one of the instruments 1 week later; 1 child completed the second instrument 3 weeks later.

Predictive Validity: Predictive Analysis 1. Thirty-five of the children who completed the Bayley-III at the initial assessment session also participated in Predictive Study 1, for which they completed a follow-up SB5 later. All 35 children in Predictive 1 were also in Predictive 2, but 5 additional children were added to Predictive 2, yielding a sample size of 40 children for this second analysis. These five children completed an initial SB5 and a follow-up SB5 but did not complete a Bayley-III. There was an 8–37 month ($Mdn = 16$ month) interval between the initial SB5 administration and the later SB5 administration. To examine the possible effect of the test-retest interval on correlations, a 16-month cut-point was used to divide the sample. The strength of the predictive correlation coefficients for the 20 participants with longer testing intervals (17–37 months) were compared to the strength of correlations for the 20 participants with shorter testing intervals (8–16 months). No comparisons were significantly different, suggesting that for the predictive studies, the longer testing intervals did not significantly reduce the strength of the correlations for pre- and post-SB5 testing.

Results

Data Processing

Data were screened for missing data points, outliers, distributional properties, and assumptions of parametric tests. No out-of-range data were discovered; no outliers were discovered using z scores > 3.29. All skewness and kurtosis statistics fell within acceptable limits (i.e., less than 2.0; Tabachnick & Fidell, 2012. Pairwise deletion methods were used when missing data were evident. Across all analyses, statistical significance was defined as $p < .05$. Refer to Table 1 for means and standard deviations of verbal, nonverbal, abbreviated, full-scale composites, and factors for both the Bayley-III and SB5.

Are Bayley-III Scores Higher than SB5 Scores?

As evident in Table 1, concurrent comparison revealed that the Bayley-III FSA tended to yield higher scores than the SB5 FSIQ (M difference $= 7.43$), $t(79) = 9.36$, $p < .001$. This pattern of significantly higher Bayley-III scores also exists when concurrently comparing the Bayley-III Cognitive Composite to the SB5 NVIQ and when comparing the Bayley-III Language Composite to the SB5 VIQ. However, in examining predictive relations, the Bayley-III FSA, Cognitive, and Language composite scores were not significantly higher than their SB5 counterparts.

Does Performance on the Bayley-III Concurrently Relate to Performance on the SB5?

Pearson product-moment correlations were calculated to determine the relation between concurrent performance on the

Bayley-III and SB5. Significant, moderate to very strong correlations were found for all relations between full-scale, verbal, and non-verbal domains on both tests, for both the clinical and comparison samples (see Table 2). All concurrent correlations between the Bayley-III and SB5 were found to be statistically significant at the $p < .001$ level. The Bayley-III FSA and the SB5 FSIQ score were strongly correlated, $r = .92$. The Bayley-III Language Composite and the SB5 VIQ score were strongly correlated, $r = .89$. The Bayley-III Cognitive Composite and the SB5 NVIQ score were strongly correlated, $r = .78$. A trend of stronger correlations for similarly defined constructs (e.g., Bayley-III Receptive Communication, Expressive Communication, and Language Composite with SB5 Knowledge and VIQ) compared to dissimilar constructs (e.g., Bayley-III Language with SB5 Visual Spatial and NVIQ) was seen. As hypothesized, the Bayley-III FSA and Language Composite correlated strongly with the SB5 Knowledge factor ($r = .88$ and $r = .88$, respectively) and Working Memory factor ($r = .83$ and $r = .80$, respectively). However, the Bayley-III FSA and Language Composite also were strongly correlated with all other SB5 factors, and the differences between factor correlations were not meaningful.

Does Performance on the Bayley-III Predict Performance on the SB5?

Performance on the Bayley-III was compared to later performance on the SB5 using Pearson product-moment correlations. Statistically significant correlations were found in comparing all domain scores from the Bayley-III to later scores on the SB5. Correlations were moderate to high in strength ($rs = .69–.80$) between full scale, verbal, and nonverbal domains (see Table 2). Given that the Bayley-III demonstrated significant correlations with the SB5 both concurrently and predictively, differences in correlation strength were of interest.

Table 2

Concurrent and Predictive Correlations, Means, and Standard Deviations for Bayley-III and SB5 for the Total Sample

	Bayley-III Full Scale Average		Bayley-III Cognitive		Bayley-III Language		Bayley-III Receptive		Bayley-III Expressive	
	Concurrent	Predictive	Concurrent	Predictive	Concurrent	Predictive	Concurrent	Predictive	Concurrent	Predictive
Correlation	n = 80	n = 35	n = 80	n = 35	n = 80	n = 35	n = 80	n = 35	n = 80	n = 35
	.92**	.80**	.77**	.76**	.90**	.74**	.86**	.72**	.89**	.71**
Bayley-III M(SD)	80.93(14.88)	84.14(16.01)	83.91(11.38)	84.97(13.01)	78.50(20.44)	83.29(21.10)	6.26(3.43)	7.06(3.80)	6.34(3.66)	7.23(3.60)
SB5 FSIQ M(SD)	73.50(17.41)	83.91(22.82)	73.50(17.41)	83.91(22.82)	73.50(17.41)	83.91(22.82)	73.50(17.41)	83.91(22.82)	73.80(17.41)	83.91(22.82)
Correlation	.85**	.76**	.78**	.75**	.80**	.69**	.77**	.67	.79**	.68**
Bayley-III M(SD)	80.93(14.88)	84.14(16.01)	83.91(11.38)	84.97(13.01)	78.50(20.44)	83.29(21.10)	6.26(3.43)	7.06(3.80)	6.34(3.66)	7.23(3.60)
SB5 NVIQ M(SD)	79.40(17.87)	86.91(23.48)	79.40(17.87)	86.91(23.48)	79.40(17.87)	86.91(23.48)	79.40(17.87)	86.91(23.48)	79.40(17.87)	86.91(23.48)
Correlation	.88**	.80**	.70**	.75**	.89**	.74**	.86**	.72**	.88**	.71**
Bayley-III M(SD)	80.93(14.88)	84.14(16.01)	83.91(11.38)	84.97(13.01)	78.50(20.44)	83.29(21.10)	6.26(3.43)	7.06(3.80)	6.34(3.66)	7.23(3.60)
SB5 VIQ M(SD)	70.74(17.26)	82.49(20.97)	70.74(17.26)	82.49(20.89)	70.74(17.26)	82.49(20.97)	70.74(17.26)	82.49(20.97)	70.74(17.26)	82.49(20.97)
Correlation	.89**	.69**	.72**	.72**	.88**	.60**	.83**	.56**	.88**	.62**
Bayley-III M(SD)	80.93(14.88)	84.14(16.01)	83.91(11.38)	84.97(13.01)	78.50(20.44)	83.29(21.10)	6.26(3.43)	7.06(3.80)	6.34(3.66)	7.23(3.60)
SB5 Abbrv M(SD)	77.80(19.46)	88.00(19.54)	77.80(19.46)	88.00(19.54)	77.80(19.46)	88.00(19.54)	77.80(19.46)	88.00(19.54)	77.80(19.46)	88.00(19.54)
Correlation	.80**	.74**	.68**	.77**	.77**	.65**	.71**	.64**	.79**	.62**
Bayley-III M(SD)	80.93(14.88)	84.14(16.01)	83.91(11.38)	84.97(13.01)	78.50(20.44)	83.29(21.10)	6.26(3.43)	7.06(3.80)	6.34(3.67)	7.23(3.60)
SB5 Fluid M(SD)	76.21(13.66)	86.11(21.10)	76.21(13.66)	86.11(21.10)	76.21(13.66)	86.11(21.10)	76.21(13.66)	86.11(21.10)	76.21(13.66)	86.11(21.10)

Concurrent and Predictive Validity of Bayley-III

Correlation	.88**	.80**	.71**	.71**	.88**	.77**	.84**	.72**	.87**	.77**
Bayley-III M(SD)	80.93(14.88)	84.14(16.01)	83.91(11.38)	84.97(13.01)	78.50(20.44)	83.29(21.10)	6.26(3.43)	7.06(3.80)	6.34(3.67)	7.23(3.60)
SB5 Know M(SD)	72.43(20.71)	83.54(19.34)	72.43(20.71)	83.54(19.34)	72.43(20.71)	83.54(19.34)	72.43(20.71)	83.54(19.34)	72.43(20.71)	83.54(19.34)
Correlation	.79**	.60**	.63**	.61**	.79**	.52*	.78**	.51**	.78**	.49**
Bayley-III M(SD)	80.93(14.88)	84.14(16.01)	83.91(11.38)	84.97(13.01)	78.50(20.44)	83.29(21.10)	6.26(3.43)	7.06(3.80)	6.34(3.67)	7.23(3.60)
SB5 Quan M(SD)	78.63(17.93)	88.60(23.27)	78.63(17.93)	88.60(23.27)	78.63(17.93)	88.60(23.27)	78.63(17.93)	88.60(23.27)	78.63(17.93)	88.60(23.27)
Correlation	.79**	.71**	.73**	.71**	.74**	.64**	.71**	.62**	.73**	.62**
Bayley-III M(SD)	80.93(14.88)	84.14(16.01)	83.91(11.38)	84.97(13.01)	78.50(20.44)	83.29(21.10)	6.26(3.43)	7.06(3.80)	6.34(3.67)	7.23(3.60)
SB5 VsSp M(SD)	81.70(14.09)	89.60(21.14)	81.70(14.09)	89.60(21.14)	81.70(14.09)	89.60(21.14)	81.70(14.09)	89.60(21.14)	81.70(14.09)	89.60(21.14)
Correlation	.83**	.71**	.72**	.72**	.80**	.81**	.78**	.79**	.78**	.78**
Bayley-III M(SD)	80.93(14.88)	84.14(16.01)	83.91(11.38)	84.97(13.01)	78.50(20.44)	83.29(21.10)	6.26(3.43)	7.06(3.80)	6.34(3.67)	7.23(3.60)
SB5 WM M(SD)	78.54(16.45)	83.91(22.33)	78.54(16.47)	83.91(22.33)	78.54(16.47)	83.91(21.10)	78.54(16.47)	83.91(21.10)	78.54(16.47)	83.91(21.10)

Note. **Bold font indicates a $p < .05$ significant difference between Bayley-III and SB5 concurrent and predictive correlations.** *Italicized bold font indicates a significant difference between Bayley-III and SB5 concurrent and predictive correlations.* FSIQ = SB5 Full Scale IQ, NVIQ = SB5 Nonverbal IQ, VIQ = SB5 Verbal IQ, Fluid = SB5 Fluid Reasoning, Know = SB5 Knowledge, Quan = SB5 Quantitative Reasoning, VsSp = SB5 Visual Spatial Processing, WM = SB5 Working Memory. Mean differences were not calculated for SB5 standard and Bayley-III scaled score comparisons.

*$p < .05$, **$p < .01$

Do Concurrent Relations and Predictive Relations Differ in Strength?

Concurrent and predictive correlations reported in Table 2 were converted to z-scores using the Fisher's r-to-z transformation, which allowed for tests of statistical significance to be conducted. Significant differences in the strength of concurrent and predictive correlations were observed for many comparisons. For all these significant differences in strength, concurrent correlations were higher than predictive correlations, indicating that the relation between performance on the Bayley-III and SB5 attenuates over time as the child ages. Correlations were significantly stronger for concurrent correlations when examining the relations between the Bayley-III FSA and the SB5 FSIQ and Abbreviated IQ; the Bayley-III Language Composite and the SB5 FSIQ, VIQ, Abbreviated IQ, and Quantitative Factor score; the Bayley-III Receptive Language score and the SB5 Abbreviated IQ and Quantitative Factor scores; and the Bayley-III Expressive Language score and the SB5 FSIQ, VIQ, Abbreviated IQ, and Quantitative Factor scores.

Are Bayley-III Scores Higher than SB5 Scores?

As evident in Table 2, concurrent comparison revealed that the Bayley-III FSA tended to yield higher scores than the SB5 FSIQ (M difference = 7.43), $t(79) = 9.36$, $p < .001$. This pattern of significantly higher Bayley-III scores also exists when concurrently comparing the Bayley-III Cognitive Composite to the SB5 NVIQ, and when comparing the Bayley-III Language Composite to the SB5 VIQ. However, in examining predictive relations, the Bayley-III FSA, Cognitive, and Language composite scores were not significantly higher than their SB5 counterparts.

Do the Bayley-III and SB5 Differentiate the Clinical Sample from the Comparison Sample?

Mean differences were significantly higher for the comparison group than the clinical group across all Bayley-III and the SB5 scores.

As expected, mean differences between groups were generally large (see Table 3).

Does Clinical Status Affect Concurrent and Predictive Relations of Bayley-III and SB5?

Concurrent correlations between scores for children who had a developmental diagnosis and children without diagnoses are displayed in Table 3. As previously described, these correlations were converted to z-scores and then compared to see whether they were significantly different from one another. The magnitude for concurrent correlations was always stronger than for predictive correlations, but only some of these differences were statistically significant. In examining concurrent relations, only three correlations were found to differ significantly based on clinical status: the correlation between the Bayley-III Cognitive Composite and the SB5 NVIQ, the correlation between the Bayley-III Cognitive Composite and the SB5 Fluid Reasoning Score, and the correlation between the Bayley-III Language Composite and the SB5 Working Memory Factor score. When examining predictive relations, three correlations were found to differ significantly based on clinical status (see Table 4): the correlations between the Bayley-III Language Composite and the SB5 VIQ; the Bayley-III Language Composite and the SB5 Quantitative Reasoning Factor score; and the Bayley-III Language Composite and the SB5 Working Memory Factor score.

Does Initial Performance on the SB5 Predictively Relate to Later Performance on the SB5?

We also explored the relationship between SB5 scores at initial testing and at a later retesting date (Predictive Analysis 2; see Table 5). The correlations between scores were strong (i.e., $r > .80$) for FSIQ, NVIQ, and VIQ for both clinical and comparison samples. Further, following a Fisher's r-to-z transformation, correlations of test-retest performance did not significantly differ from one another based on clinical/comparison group classification.

Table 3
Concurrent Correlations, Means, and Standard Deviations for Bayley-III and Stanford-Binet 5 for Clinical and Comparison Samples

	Bayley-III Full Scale Average M (SD)		Bayley-III Cognitive M (SD)		Bayley-III Language M (SD)		Bayley-III Receptive M (SD)		Bayley-III Expressive M (SD)	
	Clinical	Comparison	Clinical	Comparison	Clinical	Comparison	Clinical	Comparison	Clinical	Comparison
	n = 55	n = 25	n = 55	n = 25	n = 55	n = 25	n = 55	n = 25	n = 55	n = 25
Correlation	.78**	.87**	.58**	.75**	.75**	.83**	.68**	.69**	.70**	.84**
Bayley-III M (SD)	73.55(10.07)	97.16(10.06)	79.51(9.07)	93.60(9.95)	68.22(14.32)	101.12(11.74)	4.56(2.40)	10.00(2.14)	4.51(2.48)	10.36(2.16)
SB5 FSI M (SD)	63.78(8.12)	94.88(12.51)	63.78(8.12)	94.88(12.51)	63.78(8.12)	94.88(12.51)	63.78(8.12)	94.88(12.51)	63.78(8.12)	94.88(12.51)
Correlation	.57**	.80**	.49**	.85**	.49**	.64**	.46**	.48**	.42**	.69**
Bayley-III M (SD)	73.55(10.07)	97.16(10.06)	79.51(9.07)	93.60(9.95)	68.22(12.32)	101.12(11.74)	4.56(2.40)	10.00(2.14)	4.51(2.48)	10.36(2.16)
SB5 NVIQ M (SD)	70.20(10.66)	100.60(13.23)	70.20(10.66)	100.60(13.23)	70.20(10.66)	100.60(13.23)	70.20(10.66)	100.60(13.23)	70.20(10.66)	100.60(13.23)
Correlation	.82**	.76**	.46**	.49**	.74**	.83**	.67**	.73**	.73**	.81**
Bayley-III M (SD)	73.55(10.07)	97.16(10.06)	79.51(9.07)	93.60(9.95)	68.22(12.32)	101.12(11.74)	4.56(2.40)	10.00(2.14)	4.51(2.48)	10.36(2.16)
SB5 VIQ M (SD)	63.78(8.12)	91.15(12.50)	63.78(8.12)	91.15(12.50)	63.78(8.12)	91.15(12.50)	63.78(8.12)	91.15(12.50)	63.78(8.12)	91.15(12.50)
Correlation	.78**	.67**	.47**	.66**	.79**	.56**	.70**	.40**	.77**	.63**
Bayley-III M (SD)	73.55(10.07)	97.16(10.06)	79.51(9.07)	93.60(9.95)	68.22(12.32)	101.12(11.74)	4.56(2.40)	10.00(2.14)	4.51(2.48)	10.36(2.16)
SB5 Abbrv M (SD)	67.98(12.51)	99.40(13.02)	67.98(12.51)	99.40(13.02)	67.98(12.51)	99.40(13.02)	67.98(12.51)	99.40(13.02)	67.98(12.51)	99.40(13.02)
Correlation	.49**	.73**	.29**	.74**	.48**	.60**	.35**	.48**	.52**	.63**
Bayley-III M (SD)	73.55(10.07)	97.16(10.06)	79.51(9.07)	93.60(9.95)	68.22(12.32)	101.12(11.74)	4.56(2.40)	10.00(2.14)	4.51(2.48)	10.36(2.16)
SB5 Fluid M (SD)	69.64(8.40)	90.68(11.74)	69.64(8.40)	90.68(11.74)	69.64(8.40)	90.68(11.74)	69.64(8.40)	90.68(11.74)	69.64(8.40)	90.68(11.74)

Concurrent and Predictive Validity of Bayley-III

Correlation	.76**	.70**	.48**	.55**	.79**	.66**	.75**	.46**	.70**	.75**
Bayley-III M(SD)	73.55(10.07)	97.16(10.06)	79.51(9.07)	93.60(9.95)	68.22(12.32)	101.12(11.74)	4.56(2.40)	10.00(2.14)	4.51(2.48)	10.36(2.16)
SB5 Know M(SD)	61.60(11.19)	96.24(16.45)	61.60(11.19)	96.24(16.45)	61.60(11.19)	96.24(16.45)	61.60(11.19)	96.24(16.45)	61.60(11.19)	96.24(16.45)
Correlation	.57*	.58**	.35**	.44**	.60**	.62*	.56**	.55**	.54**	.58**
Bayley-III M(SD)	73.55(10.07)	97.16(10.06)	79.51(9.07)	93.60(9.95)	68.22(12.32)	101.12(11.74)	4.56(2.40)	10.00(2.14)	5.51(2.48)	10.36(2.16)
SB5 Quan M(SD)	69.71(7.81)	98.24(18.39)	69.71(7.81)	98.24(18.39)	69.71(7.81)	98.24(18.39)	69.71(7.81)	98.24(18.39)	69.71(7.81)	98.24(18.39)
Correlation	.52**	.72**	.48**	.70**	.41**	.59**	.39**	.52**	.41**	.57**
Bayley-III M(SD)	73.55(10.07)	97.16(10.06)	79.51(9.07)	93.60(9.95)	68.22(12.32)	101.12(11.74)	4.56(2.40)	10.00(2.14)	4.51(2.48)	10.36(2.16)
SB5 VsSpa M(SD)	75.16(9.91)	96.08(10.91)	75.16(9.91)	96.08(10.91)	75.16(9.91)	96.08(10.91)	75.16(9.91)	96.08(10.91)	75.16(9.91)	96.08(10.91)
Correlation	.52**	.73**	.50**	.56**	.43**	.74**	.40**	.66**	.37**	.71**
Bayley-III M(SD)	73.55(10.07)	97.16(10.06)	79.51(9.07)	93.60(9.95)	68.22(12.32)	101.13(11.74)	4.56(2.40)	10.00(2.14)	4.51(2.48)	10.36(2.16)
SB5 WM M(SD)	69.93(9.12)	97.48(12.63)	69.93(9.12)	97.48(12.63)	69.93(9.12)	97.48(12.63)	69.93(9.12)	97.48(12.63)	69.93(9.12)	97.48(12.63)

Note. **Bold font indicates a $p = <.05$ significant difference between Bayley-III and SB5 mean scores. *Italized bold font indicates a significant difference between the clinical and comparison samples.*** FSA = Bayley-III Full Scale Average, Cog = Bayley-III Cognitive Composite, Lang = Bayley-III Language Composite, Recpt = Bayley-III Receptive Language subtest, Expres = Bayley-III Expressive Language Subtest, FSIQ = SB5 Full Scale IQ, NVIQ = SB5 Nonverbal IQ, VIQ = SB5 Verbal IQ, Fluid = SB5 Fluid Reasoning, Know = SB5 Knowledge Index, Quan = SB5 Quantitative Reasoning, VsSpa = SB5 Visual Spatial Processing, WM = SB5 Working Memory. Mean differences were not calculated when Bayley-III scaled scores (Receptive and Expressive subscales) were compared to SB5 standard scores.
** = $p < .01$, * = $p < .05$

Table 4

Predictive Analysis 1: Correlations, Means, and Standard Deviations for Bayley-III and Stanford-Binet 5: Clinical and Comparison Samples

	Bayley-III Full Scale Average M (SD)		Bayley-III Cognitive M (SD)		Bayley-III Language M (SD)		Bayley-III Receptive M (SD)		Bayley-III Expressive M (SD)	
	Clinical	Comparison	Clinical	Comparison	Clinical	Comparison	Clinical	Comparison	Clinical	Comparison
	n = 15	n = 20	n = 15	n = 20	n = 15	n = 20	n = 15	n = 20	n = 15	n = 20
Correlation	.45	.71**	.58*	.65**	.20	.67**	.16	.56**	.22	.57**
Bayley-III M(SD)	69.67(9.85)	95.00(9.89)	76.27(11.04)	91.50(10.40)	63.07(13.00)	98.45(10.42)	3.47(2.07)	9.75(2.22)	3.93(2.46)	9.70(1.92)
SB5 FSIQ M(SD)	66.40(18.84)	97.05(15.69)	66.40(18.84)	97.05(15.69)	66.40(18.84)	97.05(15.69)	66.40(18.84)	97.05(15.96)	66.40(18.84)	97.05(15.96)
Correlation	.46	.62**	.61*	.59**	.20	.57**	.16	.47*	.23	.48*
Bayley-III M(SD)	69.67(9.85)	95.00(9.89)	76.27(11.04)	95.50(10.40)	63.07(13.00)	98.45(10.42)	3.47(2.07)	9.75(2.22)	3.93(2.46)	9.70(1.92)
SB5 NVIQ M(SD)	69.80(20.09)	99.75(16.86)	69.80(20.09)	99.75(16.86)	69.80(20.09)	99.75(16.86)	69.80(20.09)	99.75(16.86)	69.80(20.09)	99.75(16.86)
Correlation	.40	.73**	.51	.65**	.16	.71**	.13	.60**	.18	.60**
Bayley-III M(SD)	69.67(9.85)	95.00(9.89)	76.27(11.04)	91.50(10.40)	63.07(13.00)	98.45(10.42)	3.47(2.07)	9.75(2.22)	3.93(2.46)	9.70(1.92)
SB5 VIQ M(SD)	66.33(16.74)	94.60(14.83)	66.33(16.74)	94.60(14.83)	66.33(16.74)	94.60(14.83)	66.33(16.74)	94.60(14.83)	66.33(16.74)	94.60(14.83)
Correlation	.58*	.39	.69**	.47*	.31	.26	.27	.13	.33	.31
Bayley-III M(SD)	69.67(9.85)	95.00(9.89)	76.27(11.04)	91.50(10.40)	63.07(13.00)	98.45(10.42)	3.47(2.07)	9.75(2.22)	3.93(2.46)	9.70(1.29)
SB5 Abbrv M(SD)	75.40(20.79)	97.45(12.05)	75.40(20.79)	97.45(12.05)	75.40(20.79)	94.60(14.83)	75.40(20.79)	97.45(12.05)	75.40(20.79)	97.45(12.05)
Correlation	.54*	.59**	.67**	.63**	.26	.47*	.28	.39	.24	.41
Bayley-III M(SD)	69.67(9.85)	95.00(9.89)	76.72(11.04)	91.50(10.40)	63.07(13.00)	98.45(10.42)	3.47(2.07)	9.75(2.22)	3.93(2.46)	9.70(1.92)
SB5 Fluid M(SD)	72.13(18.19)	96.60(16.81)	72.13(18.19)	96.60(16.81)	72.13(18.19)	96.60(16.81)	72.13(18.19)	96.60(16.81)	72.13(18.19)	96.60(16.81)

Concurrent and Predictive Validity of Bayley-III

Correlation	.59*	.50*	.59*	.44	.40	.48*	.34	.32	.42	.50*
Bayley-III M(SD)	69.67(9.85)	95.00(9.89)	**76.27(11.04)**	91.50(10.40)	63.07(13.00)	98.45(10.42)	3.47(2.07)	9.75(2.22)	3.93(2.46)	9.70(1.92)
SB5 Know M(SD)	67.80(15.12)	95.35(12.60)	67.80(15.12)	95.35(12.60)	67.80(15.12)	95.35(12.60)	67.80(15.12)	96.60(16.81)	67.80(15.12)	95.35(12.60)
Correlation	.14	.66**	.35	.59**	-.09	**.64****	-.11	.55*	-.07	.54*
Bayley-III M(SD)	69.67(9.85)	95.00(9.89)	76.27(11.04)	**91.50(10.50)**	63.07(13.00)	98.45(10.42)	3.47(2.07)	9.75(2.22)	3.39(2.46)	9.70(1.92)
SB5 Quan M(SD)	75.60(24.55)	98.35(17.06)	75.60(24.55)	**98.35(17.06)**	75.60(24.55)	98.35(17.06)	75.60(24.55)	98.35(17.06)	75.60(24.55)	98.35(17.06)
Correlation	.52**	.68**	.61*	.59**	.28	.68**	.21	.63**	.34	.50*
Bayley-III M(SD)	**69.67(9.85)**	95.00(9.89)	76.27(11.04)	91.50(10.40)	**63.07(13.00)**	98.45(10.42)	3.47(2.07)	9.75(2.22)	3.93(2.46)	9.70(1.92)
SB5 VsSpa M(SD)	**77.47(20.97)**	98.70(16.52)	77.47(20.97)	98.70(16.52)	77.47(20.97)	98.70(16.52)	77.47(20.97)	98.70(16.52)	77.74(20.97)	98.70(16.52)
Correlation	.26	.71**	.34	.65**	.11	**.69****	.08	.57**	.14	.60**
Bayley-III M(SD)	69.67(9.85)	95.00(8.89)	**76.27(11.04)**	91.50(10.40)	63.07(13.00)	98.45(10.42)	3.47(2.07)	9.75(2.22)	3.93(2.46)	9.70(1.92)
SB5 WM M(SD)	63.60(13.72)	99.15(13.54)	**63.60(13.72)**	**99.15(13.54)**	63.60(13.72)	99.15(13.54)	63.60(13.72)	99.15(13.54)	63.60(13.72)	99.15(13.54)

Note. **Bold font indicates a significant difference between Bayley-III and SB5 mean scores.** *Italicized bold font indicates a significant difference between the clinical and comparison samples.* FSA = Bayley-III Full Scale Average, Cog = Bayley-III Cognitive Composite, Lang = Bayley-III Language Composite, Recpt = Bayley-III Receptive Language subtest, Expres = Bayley-III Expressive Language Subtest, FSIQ = SB5 Full Scale IQ, NVIQ = SB5 Nonverbal IQ, VIQ = SB5 Verbal IQ, Fluid = SB5 Fluid Reasoning, Know = SB5 Knowledge Index, Quan = SB5 Quantitative Reasoning, VsSpa = SB5 Visual Spatial Processing, WM = SB5 Working Memory. Mean differences were not calculated when Bayley-III scaled scores (Receptive and Expressive subscales) were compared to SB5 standard scores.

** $p < = .01$, * $p < = .05$

Table 5

Predictive Analysis 2: Correlations, Means, and Standard Deviations for Initial Stanford-Binet (1.SB5) and Follow-up Standford-Binet 5 (2.SB5) by Clinical (Clinic) and Comparison (Comp) Samples

	1.SBFSIQ		*1.SB5 NVIQ*		*1.SB5 VIQ*		*1.SB5 AbrvIQ*		*1.SB5 Fluid*		*1.SB5 Know*		*1.SB5 Quan*		*1.SB5 Vis Spa*		*1.SB5 WM*	
	Clinic	*Comp*	*Clinic*	*Comp*	*Clinic*	*Comp*	*Clinic*	*Comp*	*Clinic*	*Comp*	*Clinic*	*Comp*	*Clinic*	*Comp*	*Clinic*	*Comp*	*Clinic*	*Comp*
	n =18	*n* = 22	*n* =18	*n* = 22	*n* =18	*n* = 22	*n* =18	*n* = 22	*n* =18	*n* = 22	*n* =18	*n* = 22	*n* =18	*n* = 22	*n* =18	*n* = 22	*n* =18	*n* = 22
Correlation	.84**	.90**	.86**	.83**	.73**	.82**	.64**	.70**	.63**	.78**	.58**	.78**	.80**	81**	.90**	.82**	.37*	.68**
	66.00	93.18	70.89	95.73	64.28	92.05	71.56	95.77	72.22	91.18	62.00	93.73	73.39	94.41	78.72	95.91	67.94	96.41
	(11.61)	(12.23)	(12.98)	(13.38)	(10.36)	(12.63)	(15.87)	(11.99)	(11.08)	(12.89)	(11.53)	(11.33)	(20.41)	(15.56)	(15.07)	(11.66)	(8.19)	(10.57)
2. SB5 FSIQ M(SD)	71.33	99.23	71.33	99.23	71.33	99.23	71.33	99.23	71.33	99.23	71.33	99.23	71.33	99.23	71.33	99.23	71.33	99.23
	(20.41)	(16.58)	(20.41)	(16.58)	(20.41)	(16.58)	(20.41)	(16.58)	(20.41)	(16.58)	(20.41)	(16.58)	(20.41)	(16.58)	(20.41)	(16.58)	(20.41)	(16.58)
Correlation	.84**	.83**	.86**	.84**	.70**	.68**	.63**	.68**	.65**	.69**	.53**	.75**	.79**	.77**	.91**	.75**	.36**	.63**
	66.00	93.18	70.89	95.73	64.28	92.05	71.56	95.77	72.22	91.18	62.00	93.73	73.39	94.41	78.72	95.91	67.94	96.41
	(11.61)	(12.23)	(12.98)	(13.38)	(10.36)	(12.63)	(15.87)	(11.99)	(11.08)	(12.89)	(11.53)	(11.33)	(20.41)	(15.56)	(15.07)	(11.66)	(8.19)	(10.57)
2. SB5 NVIQ M(SD)	74.89	101.91	74.89	101.91	74.89	101.91	74.89	101.91	74.89	101.91	74.89	101.91	74.89	101.91	74.89	101.91	74.89	101.91
	(21.43)	(17.60)	(21.43)	(17.60)	(21.43)	(17.60)	(21.43)	(17.60)	(21.43)	(17.60)	(21.43)	(17.60)	(21.43)	(17.60)	(21.43)	(17.60)	(21.43)	(17.60)
Correlation	.83**	.89**	.83**	.75**	.73**	.88**	.62**	.65**	.58*	.80**	.63**	.73**	.79**	.77**	.86**	.82**	**.37**	**.67****
	66.00	93.18	70.89	95.73	64.28	92.05	71.56	95.77	72.22	91.18	62.00	93.73	73.39	94.41	78.72	95.91	67.94	**96.41**
	(11.61)	(12.23)	(12.98)	(13.38)	(10.36)	(12.63)	(15.87)	(11.99)	(11.08)	(12.89)	(11.53)	(11.33)	(20.41)	(15.56)	(15.07)	(11.66)	(8.19)	**(10.57)**
2. SB5 VIQ M(SD)	70.61	96.68	70.61	96.68	70.61	96.68	70.61	96.68	70.61	96.68	70.61	96.68	70.61	96.68	70.61	96.68	70.61	96.68
	(18.04)	(15.66)	(18.04)	(15.66)	(18.04)	(15.66)	(18.04)	(15.66)	(18.04)	(15.66)	(18.04)	(15.66)	(18.04)	(15.66)	(18.04)	(15.66)	(18.04)	(15.66)
Correlation	.87**	.85**	.91**	.87**	.72**	.67**	.77**	.88**	.79**	.75**	.59**	.79**	.66**	.75**	.89**	.65**	.45	.70**
	66.00	93.18	70.89	95.73	64.28	92.05	71.56	95.77	72.22	91.18	62.00	93.73	73.39	94.41	78.72	95.91	67.94	**96.41**
	(11.61)	(12.23)	(12.98)	(13.38)	(10.36)	(12.63)	(15.87)	(11.99)	(11.08)	(12.89)	(11.53)	(11.33)	(20.41)	(15.56)	(15.07)	(11.66)	(8.19)	**(10.57)**
2. SB5 Abbrev M(SD)	79.94	99.50	79.94	99.50	79.94	99.50	79.94	99.50	79.94	99.50	79.94	99.50	79.94	99.50	79.94	99.50	79.94	99.50
	(20.68)	(13.25)	(20.68)	(13.25)	(20.68)	(13.25)	(20.68)	(13.25)	(20.68)	(13.25)	(20.68)	(13.25)	(20.68)	(13.25)	(20.68)	(13.25)	(20.68)	(13.25)

Concurrent and Predictive Validity of Bayley-III

	FSIQ Clinic	FSIQ Comp	NVIQ Clinic	NVIQ Comp	VIQ Clinic	VIQ Comp	Abbrev Clinic	Abbrev Comp	Fluid Clinic	Fluid Comp	Know Clinic	Know Comp	Quan Clinic	Quan Comp	VsSpa Clinic	VsSpa Comp	WM Clinic	WM Comp
Correlation (Fluid)	.78**	.81**	.79**	.85**	.69**	.61**	.64**	.73**	.60**	.76**	.65**	.65**	.68**	.69**	.79**	.68**	.27	.60**
	66.00	93.18	70.89	95.73	64.28	92.05	71.56	95.77	72.22	91.18	62.00	93.73	73.39	94.41	78.72	95.91	67.94	96.41
	(11.61)	(12.23)	(12.98)	(13.38)	(10.36)	(12.63)	(15.87)	(11.99)	(11.08)	(12.89)	(11.53)	(11.33)	(20.41)	(15.56)	(15.07)	(11.66)	(8.19)	(10.57)
2. SB5 Fluid M(SD)	77.78	98.91	77.78	98.91	77.78	98.91	77.78	98.91	77.78	98.91	77.78	98.91	77.78	98.91	77.78	98.91	77.78	98.91
	(18.72)	(17.63)	(18.72)	(17.63)	(18.72)	(17.63)	(18.72)	(17.63)	(18.72)	(17.63)	(18.72)	(17.63)	(18.72)	(17.63)	(18.72)	(17.63)	(18.72)	(17.63)
Correlation (Know)	.81**	.82**	.84**	.78**	.71**	.73**	.79**	.75**	.69**	.69**	.70**	.91**	.58**	.77**	.81**	.66**	.48**	.66**
	66.00	93.18	70.89	95.73	64.28	92.05	71.56	95.77	72.22	91.18	62.00	93.73	73.39	94.41	78.72	95.91	67.94	96.41
	(11.61)	(12.23)	(12.98)	(13.38)	(10.36)	(12.63)	(15.87)	(11.99)	(11.08)	(12.89)	(11.53)	(11.33)	(20.41)	(15.56)	(15.07)	(11.66)	(8.19)	(10.57)
2. SB5 Know M(SD)	70.06	97.18	70.06	97.18	70.06	97.18	70.06	97.18	70.06	97.18	70.06	97.18	70.06	97.18	70.06	97.18	70.06	97.18
	(15.65)	(13.38)	(15.65)	(13.38)	(15.65)	(13.38)	(15.65)	(13.38)	(15.65)	(13.38)	(15.65)	(13.38)	(15.65)	(13.38)	(15.65)	(13.38)	(15.65)	(13.38)
Correlation (Quan)	.72**	.87**	.70**	.81**	.65**	.79**	.43	.69**	.40	.69**	.50*	.76**	.80**	.84**	.77**	.77**	.29	.68**
	66.00	93.18	70.89	95.73	64.28	92.05	71.56	95.77	72.22	91.18	62.00	93.73	73.39	94.41	78.72	95.91	67.94	96.41
	(11.61)	(12.23)	(12.98)	(13.38)	(10.36)	(12.63)	(15.87)	(11.99)	(11.08)	(12.89)	(11.53)	(11.33)	(20.41)	(15.56)	(15.07)	(11.66)	(8.19)	(10.57)
2. SB5 Quan M(SD)	79.89	100.73	79.89	100.73	79.89	100.73	79.89	100.73	79.89	100.73	79.89	100.73	79.89	100.73	79.89	100.73	79.89	100.73
	(25.42)	(18.15)	(25.42)	(18.15)	(25.42)	(18.15)	(25.42)	(18.15)	(25.42)	(18.15)	(25.42)	(18.15)	(25.42)	(18.15)	(25.42)	(18.15)	(25.42)	(18.15)
Correlation (VsSpa)	.75**	.73**	.82**	.64**	.56**	.71**	.60**	.45**	.58**	.65**	.35	.56**	.68**	.63**	.90**	.81**	.38	.48*
	66.00	93.18	70.89	95.73	64.28	92.05	71.56	95.77	72.22	91.18	62.00	93.73	73.39	94.41	78.72	95.91	67.94	96.41
	(11.61)	(12.23)	(12.98)	(13.38)	(10.36)	(12.63)	(15.87)	(11.99)	(11.08)	(12.89)	(11.53)	(11.33)	(20.41)	(15.56)	(15.07)	(11.66)	(8.19)	(10.57)
2. SB5 VsSpa M(SD)	80.89	100.23	80.89	100.23	80.89	100.23	80.89	100.23	80.89	100.23	80.89	100.23	80.89	100.23	80.89	100.23	80.89	100.23
	(19.96)	(16.53)	(19.96)	(16.53)	(19.96)	(16.53)	(19.96)	(16.53)	(19.96)	(16.53)	(19.96)	(16.53)	(19.96)	(16.53)	(19.96)	(16.53)	(19.96)	(16.53)
Correlation (WM)	.73**	.79**	.72**	.62**	.62**	.82**	.43	.51*	.59**	.66**	.39	.60**	.74**	.68**	.71**	.73**	.32*	.66**
	66.00	93.18	70.89	95.73	64.28	92.05	71.56	95.77	72.22	91.18	62.00	93.73	73.39	94.41	78.72	95.91	67.94	96.41
	(11.61)	(12.23)	(12.98)	(13.38)	(10.36)	(12.63)	(15.87)	(11.99)	(11.08)	(12.89)	(11.53)	(11.33)	(20.41)	(15.56)	(15.07)	(11.66)	(8.19)	(10.57)
2. SB5 WM M(SD)	69.11	100.41	69.11	100.41	69.11	100.41	69.11	100.41	69.11	100.41	69.11	100.41	69.11	100.41	69.11	100.41	69.11	100.41
	(16.37)	(13.68)	(16.37)	(13.68)	(16.37)	(13.68)	(16.37)	(13.68)	(16.37)	(13.68)	(16.37)	(13.68)	(16.37)	(13.68)	(16.37)	(13.68)	(16.37)	(13.68)

Note. **All Clinical and Comparison scores were significantly different.** Clinic = Clinical sample, Comp = Comparison sample, FSIQ = SB5 Full Scale IQ, NVIQ = SB5 Nonverbal IQ, VIQ = SB5 Verbal IQ, Abbrev = Abbreviated IQ, Fluid = SB5 Fluid Reasoning, Know = SB5 Knowledge Index, Quan = SB5 Quantitative Reasoning, VsSpa = SB5 Visual Spatial Processing, WM = SB5 Working Memory.

** $p <= .01$, * $p <= .05$

Does the SB5 Differentiate the Clinical Sample from the Comparison Sample at Initial and Follow-up testing?

Mean differences were significantly higher for the comparison group than the clinical group across all SB5 scores. As expected, mean differences between groups were generally large (see Table 5).

Discussion

It is often theorized that the nature of cognitive and developmental functioning may change across the lifespan, which necessitates study as to whether developmental and cognitive functioning instruments are measuring the same construct at different ages and times. In this study, two instruments, the Bayley-III and the SB5, were administered to a racially and ethnically diverse sample of 85 very young children, and the relations between their scores were examined. Despite the Bayley-III often yielding statistically higher scores than the SB5, this study lends support to theory that the Bayley-III and SB5 are measuring similar constructs in that correlations of like constructs were strong, with only a few exceptions.

The Bayley-III FSA and SB5 FSIQ

Although no overall composite for the Bayley-III is typically yielded from testing, the average of the cognitive and language domains of the Bayley-III, suggested by Moore et al. (2012) and called the FSA in the current study, appears to be a useful metric supported by validity evidence. When considering the total sample and concurrent correlations, consistent with our hypotheses, results revealed that the Bayley-III FSA strongly correlated with SB5 FSIQ ($r = .92$). Correlations did not differ in strength for the clinical and comparison samples. This correlation also remained strong when examining the predictive relation between the two measures ($r = .80$).

It was further hypothesized that the Bayley-III would yield statistically significantly higher scores than the SB5. The Bayley-III yielded higher concurrent Bayley-III FSA scores than the SB5 FSIQ for the sample as a whole (a mean difference of 7.43). However, mean differences decreased dramatically in examining predictive relations, as the Bayley-III FSA was on average only 0.23 points higher than the SB5 FSIQ when tested at follow-up months later.

Our hypothesis that the Bayley-III Language Composite and related Bayley-III scores would strongly correlate with the SB5 VIQ was also supported. The Language Composite scores demonstrated both strong concurrent ($r = .89$) and predictive ($r = .74$) relations. The consistently low correlations reported by Kamppi and Gilmore (2010) were not seen in our clinical sample. Moreover, the Bayley-III Language Composite was strongly associated with other SB5 composites and factors for our comparison sample. The same result was not found by Kamppi and Gilmore (2010), although both the Kamppi and Gilmore sample and our sample were of similar size. Statistically stronger associations were also demonstrated for Bayley-III Language Composite and the SB5 FSIQ, NVIQ, VIQ, and Fluid Reasoning and Working Memory factors than reported in the Kamppi and Gilmore study. Our hypothesis that the Bayley-III Language Composite would yield higher scores than the SB5 Verbal Composite was also supported, as the combined sample scored 7.76 points higher on the Bayley-III Language Composite when examining concurrent relations. However, no meaningful mean differences were apparent when examining predictive relations.

Our hypothesis that the Bayley-III Cognitive Composite would strongly correlate with the SB5 NVIQ was supported. Both strong concurrent ($r = .78$) and predictive ($r = .75$) relations were demonstrated. The Bayley-III Cognitive Composite was more strongly associated with the SB5 FSIQ than was found by Kamppi and Gilmore (2010). Further, associations between the Bayley-III Cognitive Composite and SB5 NVIQ, the Bayley-III Cognitive Composite and SB5 Fluid Reasoning Factor score, and the Bayley-III Cognitive Composite and SB5 Visual-Spatial Reasoning Factor score were stronger than the associations observed by Kamppi and Gilmore (2010). However, our hypothesis that the Bayley-III Cognitive Composite would yield higher scores than the SB5 NVIQ was not fully supported. Children did in fact score on average 4.51 points higher on the Bayley-III Cognitive Composite than on the SB5 NVIQ when examining concurrent relations, but scored 1.94 points higher on the SB5 NVIQ than on the Bayley-III Cognitive Composite when examining predictive relations.

When considering the five SB5 factors, we hypothesized that the Bayley-III FSA would correlate most strongly with the SB5 Knowledge and Working Memory factors. The Bayley-III FSA was strongly correlated with both factor scores when examining concurrent relations (.88 and .83, respectively) and when examining predictive relations (.80 and .83). While the Bayley-III FSA's strongest correlations were the strongest with Knowledge and Working Memory, these correlations were not significantly stronger than other correlations with the SB5 factors.

Of interest to practitioners is whether certain abbreviated assessments (e.g., the SB5 ABIQ) can accurately identify children with developmental delays (Twomey, O'Connell, Lillis, Tarpey, & O'Reilly, 2018). Twomey et al. (2018) found that the SB5 ABIQ has a strong correlation ($r = .89$) with the SB5 FSIQ. Similarly, we found strong concurrent and predictive associations between the SB5 ABIQ and the Bayley-III FSA with correlations of $r = .89$ and $r = .69$, respectively. These correlations tended to be slightly stronger for children in the clinical sample than for children in the comparison sample. We also found strong predictive associations between the initial SB5 ABIQ and the follow-up FSIQ for both the clinical and comparison samples, with correlations of $r = .87$ and $r = .85$, respectively.

Milne et al. (2012) found that the Bayley-III was a better predictor of future cognitive performance for children of lower intellectual ability than for children of average intellectual ability. Contrary to these findings, the Bayley-III was found to predict future cognitive performance on the SB5 for children with no known disabilities as well as for children with a diagnosis of a developmental disability.

Limitations

Many of the limitations of this study pertain to its methodology, especially as they relate to the samples and procedure used in this study. The sample used in this study was divided into a clinical sample and a comparison sample with an overrepresentation of African American and male participants. Further, the DD sample was heavily weighted with children with ASD in the clinical samples (69% concurrent clinical; 83% of predictive clinical samples). It is possible that a diagnosis of ASD may interact differently with IQ, both concurrently and predictively, than the other diagnoses present in the clinical sample. As the sample was divided into clinical and comparison groups and further subdivided into participants with concurrent and predictive validity study data, the limited number of participants in some groups made it difficult to detect statistically significant differences in correlations across groups. The restricted range in IQs of the comparison group presented a limitation, as there were relatively few children demonstrating high levels of performance.

When examining predictive validity, the gap between initial assessment with the Bayley-III and subsequent assessment with the SB5 varied considerably (from 8–37 months). Future research involving these two instruments should examine predictive validity continuously across time (rather than as a binary variable in comparison with concurrent validity). Our study did not have the statistical power to carry out such continuous analysis. Further, as most of the children in the clinical sample were enrolled in interventions such as ABA between initial testing and follow-up testing, interventions may have resulted in IQ gains. Research has extensively documented that ABA therapy can result in IQ gains (Lovaas, 1987; Smith, Groen, & Wynn, 2000), especially when employed as an early intervention strategy.

A further limitation of this study is that the validity of only two measures, the Bayley-III and the SB5, was examined. Future research may seek to relate performance on one or both measures to other assessments of cognitive ability (e.g., the Wechsler scales), to assessments of adaptive ability, or to other assessments of socioemotional functioning.

Conclusions

Although both the Bayley-III and SB5 are frequently used cognitive instruments, few studies have concurrently compared preschoolers' performances using these assessments, and fewer yet have examined how the two assessments relate predictively to one another. This study addressed this under-researched area utilizing a diverse sample. Results suggest that the two instruments are measuring the same cognitive and developmental constructs. Although Bayley-III scores are generally higher than SB5 scores, both differentiated comparison from clinical groups. However, as recommended by Moore et al. (2012), the trend toward higher Bayley-III scores suggests the need for somewhat higher cut-points when used as a screening tool for at-risk populations. More research is needed to examine more fully predictive associations with later SB5 administration. Yet, with this limited sample, support is provided for the Bayley-III being a good predictor of later IQ testing during the preschool years. Likewise, the SB5 is a very strong predictor of follow-up SB5 scores for this sample of young children.

Authors' Note

This research was partially funded by DHHS-HRSA Grant MC-0038. The authors wish to thank Jessica Myszak, Lauren Gardner, Phil Norfolk, Tera Bradley, Aimee Rovane, Ashley Dillon, Sarah Irby, and Bruce Keisling for their assistance with the project. The authors would also like to thank the children and caregivers who participated in the research.

References

Acton, B. V., Biggs, W. S. G., Creighton, D. E., Penner, K. A. H., Switzer, H. N., Thomas, J. H. P., ... Robertson, C. M. T. (2011). Overestimation of neurodevelopment using Bayley-III after complex cardiac surgery. *Journal of Pediatrics, 12,* 84, e794–800.

Alfonso, V. C., & Flanagan, D. P. (2007) Best practices in the use of the Stanford-Binet Intelligence Scales, Fifth Edition (SB5) with preschoolers. In B. A. Bracken & R. J. Nagle (Eds.), *Psychoeducational assessment of preschool children* (4th ed., pp. 267–296). Mahway, NJ: Erlbaum.

American Psychiatric Association. (2013). *Diagnostic and statistical manual of mental disorders* (5th ed.). Washington, DC: Author.

Anderson, P. J., & Burnett, A. (2017). Assessing developmental delays in early childhood-concerns with the Bayley-III Scales. *The Clinical Neuropsychologist, 31*(2), 371–381.

Anderson, P. J., Deluca, C. R., Hutchinson, E., Roberts, G., & Doyle, L. W. (2010). Victorian Infants Collaborative Group: Underestimation of developmental delay by the New Bayley-III Scale. *Archives of Pediatric and Adolescent Psychiatry, 164,* 352–356.

Aylward, G. P. (2009). Developmental screening and assessment: What are we thinking? *Journal of Developmental and Behavioral Pediatrics, 30,* 169–173.

Bayley, N. (1993). *Bayley Scales of Infant Development, Second Edition.* San Antonio, TX; Psychological Corporation.

Bayley, N. (2005). *Bayley Scales of Infant and Toddler Development, Third Edition.* San Antonio, TX: Psychological Corporation/Pearson.

Bayley, N. (2006a). *Bayley Scales of Infant and Toddler Development, Third Edition administration manual.* San Antonio, TX: Psychological Corporation/Pearson.

Bayley, N. (2006b). *Bayley Scales of Infant and Toddler Development, Third Edition technical manual.* San Antonio, TX: Psychological Corporation/Pearson.

Becker, K. A. (2003). *History of the Stanford-Binet Intelligence Scales: Content and psychometrics.* (Stanford-Binet Intelligences Scales, Fifth Edition Assessment Service Bulletin No. 1). Itasca, IL: Riverside Publishing.

Bode, M. M., D'Eugenio, D. B., Mettelman, B. B., & Gross, S. J. (2014). Predictive validity of the Bayley, Third Edition at 2 years for intelligence quotient at 4 years for preterm infants. *Journal of Developmental Behavioral Pediatrics, 35,* 570–575.

Bos, A.F. (2013). Bayley-II or Bayley-III: What do the scores tell us? *Developmental Medicine & Child Neurology, 55,* 973–979.

Bracken, B. A. (1987). Limitations of preschool instruments and standards for minimal levels of technical adequacy. *Journal of Psychoeducational Assessment, 4,* 313–326.

Bracken, B. A., & Nagle, R. J. (Eds.). (2007). *Psychoeducational assessment of preschool children* (4th ed.). Mahway, NJ: Erlbaum.

Bracken, B. A., & Walker, K. C. (1997). The utility of intelligence tests for preschool children. In D. P. Flanagan, J. L. Genshaft, & P. L. Harrison (Eds.), *Contemporary* intellectual assessment: Theories, tests, and issues (pp. 484–505). New York, NY: Guilford Press.

Bradley-Johnson, S., & Durmusoglu, G. (2005). Evaluation of floors and item gradients for reading and math tests for young children. *Journal of Psychoeducational Assessment, 23,* 262–278.

Bradley-Johnson, S., & Johnson, C. M. (2007). Infant and toddler cognitive assessment. In B. A. Bracken & R. J. Nagle (Eds.), *Psychoeducational assessment of preschool children* (4th ed., pp. 325–358). Mahway, NJ: Erlbaum.

Brassard, M. R., & Boehm, A. E. (2007). *Preschool assessment: Principles and practices.* New York, NY: Guilford Press.

Camara, W. J., Nathan, J. S., & Puente, A. E. (2000). Psychological test use: Implications in professional psychology. *Professional Psychology: Research and Practice, 31,* 141–154.

Chinta, S., Walker, K., Halliday, R., Loughran-Fowlds, A., & Bawadi, N. (2014). A comparison of the performance of healthy Australian 3-year-olds with the standardized norms of the Bayley Scales of Infant and Toddler Development (Version-III). *Archives of Disease in Childhood, 99*(7), 621–624.

Elliott, C. D. (2007). *Differential Ability Scales, Second Edition.* San Antonio, TX: Harcourt Assessment.

Finello, K. M. (2011). Collaboration in the assessment and diagnosis of preschoolers: Challenges and opportunities. *Psychology in the Schools, 48,* 442–453.

Geisinger, K .F., Spies, R. A., Carlson, J. F., & Plake, B. S. (Eds.). (2007). *The seventeenth mental measurements yearbook.* Lincoln, NE: Buros Institute of Mental Measurements.

Jary, S., Whitelaw, A., Walloe, L., & Thoreson, M. (2013). Comparison of Bayley-2 and Bayley-III scores at 18 months in term infants following neonatal encephalopathy and therapeutic hypothermia. *Developmental Medicine & Child Neurology, 55,* 1053–1059.

Johnson, S., Moore, T., & Marlow, N. (2014). Using the Bayley-III to assess neurodevelopmental delay. Which cut-off should be used? *Pediatric Research, 75,* 670–674.

Kamppi, D., & Gilmore, L. (2010). Assessing cognitive development in early childhood: A comparison of the Bayley-III and the Stanford-Binet Fifth Edition. *Australian Educational and Developmental Psychologist, 27*(2), 70–75.

Kaplan, R. M., & Saccuzzo, D.P. (Eds.). (2017). *Psychological testing: Principles, applications, and issues* (9th ed.). Boston, MA: Cengage Learning.

Long, S. H., Galea, M. P., Eldridge, B. J., & Harris, S. R. (2012). Performance of 2-year-old children after surgery for congenital heart disease on the Bayley Scales of

Infant and Toddler Development, Third Edition. *Early Human Development, 88*(8), 603–607.

Lovaas, O. I. (1987). Behavioural treatment and normal educational and intellectual functioning in young autistic children. *Journal of Consulting and Clinical Psychology, 55,* 3–9

Milne, S., McDonald, J., & Comino, E. (2012). The use of the Bayley Scales of Infant and Toddler Development III with clinical populations: A preliminary exploration. *Physical & Occupational Therapy in Pediatrics, 32*(1), 24–33.

Molfese, V. J., & Acheson, S. (1997). Infant and preschool mental and verbal abilities: How are infant scores related to preschool scores? *International Journal of Behavioral Development, 20,* 595–607.

Moore, T., Johnson, S., Haider, S., Hennessey, E., & Marlow, N. (2012). Relationship between test scores of the second and third editions of the Bayley Scales in extremely preterm children. *Journal of Pediatrics, 160,* 553–558.

Nagle, R.J. (2000). Issues in preschool assessment. In B. A. Bracken (Ed.), *The psychoeducational assessment of preschool children* (3rd ed., pp 19–32). Boston, MA: Allyn & Bacon.

Nagle, R. J. (2017). Issues in preschool assessment. In B. A. Bracken & R. J. Nagle (Eds.), *Psychoeducational assessment of preschool children* (4th ed., pp. 36). Mahwah, NJ: Erlbaum.

Neisser, U., Boodoo, G., Bouchard, T. J., Jr., Boykin, A. W., Brody, N., Ceci, S. J., ... Urbina, S. (1996). Intelligence: Knowns and unknowns. *American Psychologist, 51*(2), 77–101.

Roid, G. H. (2003a). *Stanford-Binet Intelligence Scales, Fifth Edition.* Rolling Meadows, IL: Riverside Publishing.

Roid, G .H. (2003b). *Stanford-Binet Intelligence Scales, Fifth Edition examiner's manual.* Rolling Meadows, IL: Riverside Publishing.

Roid, G. H., (2003c). *Stanford-Binet Intelligence Scales, Fifth Edition technical manual.* Rolling Meadows, IL: Riverside Publishing.

Rubio-Codina, M., Araujo, M. C., Attanasio, O., Munoz, P., & Grantham-McGregor, S. (2016). Concurrent validity and feasibility of short tests currently used to measure early childhood development in large scale studies. *PLoS ONE, 11*(8), e0160962.

Sattler, J. M. (2008). *Assessment of children: Cognitive foundations* (5th ed.). San Diego, CA: Author.

Scattone, D., Raggio, D. J., & May, W. (2011). Comparison of the Vineland Adaptive Behavior Scales, Second Edition, and the Bayley Scales of Infant and Toddler Development (3rd ed.). *Psychological Reports, 109*(2), 626–634.

Silveira, R. C., Filipouski, G. R., Goldstein, D. J., O'Shea, T., & Procianoy, R. S. (2012). Agreement between Bayley Scales second and third edition assessments of very low-birth-weight infants. *Archives of Pediatric & Adolescent Medicine, 166,* 1075–1076.

Smith, T., Groen, A.D., & Wynn, J.W. (2000). Randomized trial of intensive early intervention for children with pervasive developmental disorder. *American Journal on Mental Retardation, 105*(4), 269-285.

Spencer-Smith, M. M., Spittle, A. J., Lee, K. J., Doyle, L. W., & Anderson, P. J. (2015). Bayley-III Cognitive and Language Scales in preterm children. *Pediatrics, 135*(5), 1258–1265.

Sternberg, R. J., Grigorenko, E. L., & Bundy, D. A. (2001). The predictive value of IQ. *Merrill-Palmer Quarterly, 47,* 1–41.

Tabachnick, B. G., & Fidell, L. S. (2012). *Using multivariate statistics* (6th ed.). New York, NY: Pearson.

Twomey, C., O'Connell, H., Lillis, M., Tarpey, S. L., & O'Reilly, G. (2018). Utility of an abbreviated version of the Stanford-Binet Intelligence Scales (5th ed.) in estimating "full scale" IQ for young children with autism spectrum disorder. *Autism Research, 11*(3), 503–508.

Vig, S., & Sanders, M. (2007). Cognitive assessment. In M. R. Brassard & A. E. Boehm (Eds.), *Preschool assessment: Principles and practices* (pp. 394–396). New York, NY: Guilford Press.

Vohr, B. R., Stephens, B. E., Higgins, R. D., Bann, C. M., Hintz, S. R., Das, A., ... Fuller, J. (2012). Are outcomes of extremely preterm infants improving? Impact of Bayley assessment on outcomes. *Journal of Pediatrics, 161*(2), 222–228, e3.

Wechsler, D. (2002). *Wechsler Preschool and Primary Scale of Intelligence* (3rd ed.). San Antonio, TX: Psychological Corporation.

Weisglas-Kuperus, N., Baerts, W., & Sauer, P. J. (1993). Early assessment and neurodevelopmental outcome in very low-birth-weight infants: Implications for pediatric practice. *Acta Paediatrica, 82,* 449–453.

Yu, Y. T., Hsieh, W. S., Hsu, C. H., Chen, L. C., Lee, W. T., Chiu, N. C., ... Jeng, S. F. (2013). A psychometric study of the Bayley Scales of Infant and Toddler Development: Third edition for term and preterm Taiwanese infants. *Research in Developmental Disabilities, 34*(11), 3875–3883.

Psychometric Properties of a Kindergarten Readiness Assessment Using Exploratory Structural Equation Modeling

Annie C. Liner, Kathryn L. Fletcher, and Patricia C. Clark

Abstract

This study examined the construct, concurrent, and predictive validity of the Essential Skills kindergarten readiness assessment (ESKRA). Using the National Education Goal Panel's (NEGP) five dimensions of kindergarten readiness, we examined a five-factor solution for construct validity. Controlling for children's demographics, one of the factors, literacy, from the five-factor solution, predicted kindergarten children's reading and math scores at the beginning of the kindergarten year. High levels of reliability were found for each of the five discovered factors. Establishing community-level kindergarten readiness through reliable assessments impacts targeting community initiatives to increase kindergarten readiness, such as efforts to improve the quality of child care programs and engage families in their children's early learning and development.

Keywords: kindergarten assessment, school readiness, five readiness domains, kindergarten transition

Kindergarten is a critical milestone that nearly four million children between the ages of 5 and 6 embark upon in the fall of each new school year in the United States (U.S. Department of Education, 2015). Children's transition to kindergarten is an important first step in their educational careers. Many school districts assess children's "readiness" at the start of kindergarten (Forry & Wessel, 2012; Kagan, Moore, & Bradekamp, 1995; Texas Early Learning Council, 2011). Kindergarten readiness is a finite construct that assumes children will have the minimum levels of skills in cognitive, physical, and social and emotional development to be ready to benefit from kindergarten instruction (Kagan & Rigby, 2003; Scott-Little, Kagan, & Frelow, 2006). Although there is no universal definition of kindergarten readiness (Graue, 1993; Gredler, 1992; Snow, 2006), educators and policymakers agree that kindergarten readiness is multidimensional (Gullo, 2015; Heckman, 2006; Kagan et al., 1995; Wakabayashi & Beal, 2015).

The National Educational Goal Panel (NEGP) in 1990 introduced the multidimensional framework that has become the prominent theoretical framework for evaluating kindergarten readiness (Kagan et al., 1995). Five dimensions of readiness outlined by the NEGP included physical well-being and motor development; social and emotional development; approaches toward learning; language development; and cognition (Kagan et al., 1995). Based on the five dimensions of readiness framework, many children fall short of meeting minimum skills in these areas; thus, they are considered "not ready" for kindergarten (Child Trends, 2001). Children who are assessed as behind in kindergarten readiness skills remain behind in academic achievement in later school years (Grimm, Steele, Mashburn, Burchinal, & Pianta, 2010; Lloyd & Hertzman, 2009). To inform community initiatives involving early childhood programs and family involvement, it is imperative to accurately assess children's developmental skills when they enter kindergarten using valid and reliable assessments.

Although there are a wide variety of kindergarten readiness assessments used across different communities, only a few are valid and reliable instruments (Carney & Merrell, 2002; Meisels, Henderson,

Liaw, Browning, & Have, 1993). Specifically, the assessment should be appropriate, meaningful, and serve the purpose intended while providing consistent results from one administration to the next (Duncan & Rafter, 2005; Snow & Van Hemel, 2008). The concept of assessing young children for kindergarten readiness is controversial. However, without validity and reliability evidence for kindergarten readiness assessments, it will remain difficult to accurately evaluate children's kindergarten readiness. Using exploratory structural equation modeling to assess the validity of a locally-developed kindergarten readiness assessment, the current study examined the validity and reliability of a district-wide kindergarten readiness assessment.

The NEGP acknowledged that kindergarten readiness should encompass five dimensions: physical well-being and motor development; social and emotional development; approaches toward learning; language development; and cognition and general knowledge (Kagan et al., 1995). In the mid-1990s, the proposal for these five dimensions of kindergarten readiness and their relationship to academic achievement were based on the available research at the time (Kagan et al., 1995). Over the last two decades, research on kindergarten readiness has greatly expanded. Studies that ranged from examining the predictability of one dimension on later academic achievement (Blair, 2001; Cameron et al., 2012; Lonigan et al., 2015) to national longitudinal studies that have sought to verify models of kindergarten readiness have been conducted (Snow, 2006). To our knowledge, the United Kingdom, Canada, and the United States have conducted large-scale longitudinal studies that have provided information about children's developmental skills before or during their kindergarten year and academic achievement in later elementary school years. Controlling for child and family demographic variables, this body of research on how kindergarten readiness skills predicts academic achievement has provided substantial empirical support for the multidimensional model of kindergarten readiness (Duncan et al., 2007; Grissmer, Grimm, Aiyer, Murrah, & Steele, 2010; Hooper, Roberts,

Sideris, Burchinal, & Zeisel, 2010; Pagani, Fitzpatrick, Archambault, & Janosz, 2010; Romano, Babchishin, Pagani, & Kohen, 2010).

Children's language, cognition, and approaches to learning in kindergarten have been consistent predictors of academic achievement in later elementary school years. Assessment items related to approaches to learning have focused on children's attention skills. Children's attention and concentration have long been established as robust predictors of later reading and math outcomes for children during the elementary school years (Blair & Razza, 2007; Pagani & Fitzpatrick, 2014; Tramontana, Hooper, & Selzer, 1988; Welsh, Nix, Blair, Bierman, & Nelson, 2010). Using national data sets with subjective (i.e., teachers' and parents' ratings) as well as objective (i.e., task persistence) measures of attention skills, children's high levels of attention were associated with high scores in math and reading outcomes, but this association was not found in two national samples (Duncan et al., 2007; Hooper et al., 2010; Romano et al., 2010). In contrast, children's attention problems consistently yielded a negative association with achievement outcomes for second graders (Pagani et al., 2010), third graders (Duncan et al., 2007; Grissmer et al., 2010), and fifth graders (Duncan et al., 2007; Grissmer et al., 2010). Similar to children's attention problems, children's language and literacy skills as well as their number skills (i.e., cognitive/ general knowledge domain) predicted children's later reading and math achievement (Duncan et al., 2007; Hooper et al., 2010; Kurdek & Sinclair, 2001; Pagani & Fitzpatrick, 2014; Pagani et al., 2010; Romano et al., 2010; Tramontana et al., 1988). Using national data sets, direct assessments of kindergarten children's reading and math skills were consistently associated with later reading and math outcomes across grade levels (Duncan et al., 2007; Grissmer et al., 2010; Hooper et al., 2010; Pagani et al., 2010; Romano et al., 2010).

Empirical findings related to kindergarten children's gross motor skills and social and emotional skills as predictors of academic achievement have been less consistent than the other three dimensions. Kindergarten children's gross motor skills either had a negative relationship or no relationship to reading outcomes, whereas children's fine motor skills in kindergarten positively predicted later reading and math outcomes (Cameron et al., 2012; Grissmer et al., 2010; Pagani et al., 2010). In contrast to the other four readiness domains, children's social and emotional development is more difficult to directly observe, meaning that researchers must rely on parents' and/or teachers' reports of children's behaviors. Furthermore, parents' and/or teachers' ratings for different aspects of children's social and emotional development such as externalizing behaviors, internalizing behaviors, and prosocial behaviors have been used. Examining teachers' ratings of children's prosocial skills, emotional distress, and aggression, children's prosocial skills predicted fourth grade reading scores, but teachers' ratings of children's physical aggression and emotional distress did not (Pagani & Fitzpatrick, 2014). Although there were some nuanced positive findings across studies using national data sets, kindergarten children's social skills, internalizing behaviors, and externalizing behaviors were less consistent significant predictors of later reading and math achievement (Duncan et al., 2007; Grissmer et al., 2010; Hooper et al., 2010; Pagani et al., 2010; Romano et al., 2010). Despite these findings, the debate continues regarding the significance of children's social and emotional skills for kindergarten readiness, with some researchers suggesting an indirect relationship between social behaviors and later achievement outcomes through approaches to learning (Bierman, Domitrovich, Nix, Welsh & Gest, 2008; Ladd, Buhs, & Seid, 2000). Although research findings might be inconsistent for some readiness skills, to date, empirical support exists for using assessment items that examine children's skills within the five dimensions of kindergarten readiness.

Developing kindergarten readiness assessments involving these five dimensions has become important to community efforts to evaluate the effectiveness of services and programming to increase children's kindergarten readiness skills. Evaluating the effectiveness of these community initiatives has been complicated, however, because there are no universal kindergarten screening assessments, and few of the available assessments are valid and reliable (Carney & Merrell, 2002; Meisels et al., 1993). According to the position paper of the National Association for the Education of Young Children and National Association of Early Childhood Specialists in State Departments of Education (2003), assessments of young children must be valid, reliable, and used for an intended purpose. For the purpose of this research, we sought to establish the validity and reliability of an instrument for kindergarten readiness that was intended to gauge community-wide levels of kindergarten readiness, rather than instructional or educational decisions about individual children. Assessments must be valid and reliable in order to evaluate the efforts of local community initiatives (Duncan & Rafter, 2005; Quirk, Mayworm, Edyburn, & Furlong, 2016; Snow & Van Hemel, 2008). Without valid and reliable assessments for kindergarten readiness, it will remain difficult to accurately evaluate the success of community efforts to increase the number of children ready for kindergarten. The purpose of this study was to examine the reliability and validity of the ESKRA, a 23-item instrument based on teacher ratings designed to assess children's kindergarten readiness skills. It is important to note that ESKRA has never been used to make instructional or educational decisions for individual children. Instead, it is used to assess the effectiveness of community level early childhood programming. In the current study, the following questions were examined: (a) What is the construct validity of the ESKRA? (b) What is the concurrent validity of the ESKRA? (c) Does the ESKRA predict kindergarten math and reading outcomes? and (d) What is the reliability of the ESKRA?

Methods

Participants

Data were collected on 475 kindergarten children from a local school district in the mid-west. Twenty-one kindergarten teachers in the district completed the ESKRA for every kindergarten student in their classroom during the first month of school. Of the 475 children, the majority of the kindergarten students were White (63%) and about half of the students were males (53%). The majority of the kindergarten students received free lunch or reduced fee lunch (79%). Lunch status was used as a proxy for family income, with free or reduced lunch fees indicating lower income households. Fifty-three percent of the kindergarten students had previous preschool experience, 33% did not attend preschool before kindergarten, and the remaining 14% preschool experience was unknown.

Measures

Essential Skills kindergarten readiness assessment. Items for the ESKRA were selected in consultation with kindergarten teachers from the school district from a larger set of items that were proposed based on research with teachers from across the state. Eight teachers completed the Essential Skills for Successful School Readiness survey (ESSSR; Conn-Powers, 2008). The ESSSR is comprised of 70 items on skills related to the five dimensions of kindergarten readiness and teachers were instructed to rate the importance (i.e., not important, important, critical) of each kindergarten readiness skill. Items that received a rating of critical or important and were endorsed by at least 75% of the teachers were retained for the ESKRA. Although not selected by the teachers, the decision was made to add three literacy items to the assessment. This resulted in a 23-item assessment, with a 4-point Likert like rating scale: (1) rarely, (2) sometimes, (3) usually, and (4) always. The assessment consisted of the following: (a) three items represented approaches to learning, (b) three items represented cognition and general knowledge, (c) 10 items represented language and literacy, (d) two items represented physical development, and (e) five items represented social and emotional development.

DIBELS Math. The Dynamic Indicators of Basic Early Literacy Skills (DIBELS) math assesses entry-level math skills as well as gains in math skills from kindergarten through sixth grade. In this local school district, the DIBELS math assessment was administered to kindergarteners three times during the school year: fall, winter, and spring. Students' fall math composite scores, consisting of counting, number identification, missing number, and quantity discrimination items, were combined for a total score and then used to control for entry-level math skills. Students' spring math subscale scores, consisting of the same subscales used at the beginning of the year measure, were combined for a total score and used to examine predictive validity.

DIBELS Next. The Dynamic Indicators of Basic Early Literacy Skills (DIBELS Next) measures entry-level literacy skills as well as the gains in early literacy from kindergarten through sixth grade. In this local school district, the DIBELS reading assessment was administered to kindergarteners three times a school year: fall, winter, and spring. Students' fall reading composite scores (i.e., subscales of first sound frequency and letter naming fluency) were used to control for entry level reading skills. Students' spring reading subscale scores (i.e., subscales of phoneme segmentation fluency, nonsense word fluency with correct letter sounds, and nonsense word fluency with whole words read) were combined for a total reading score and used to examine predictive validity.

Results

The data analysis was conducted using the Statistical Package Mplus version 7.11 to perform an Exploratory Structural Equation Model (ESEM) to examine the construct validity of the instrument. ESEM integrates features of exploratory factor analysis, confirmatory factor analysis, and structural equation modeling (SEM) that allows for exploratory investigations of factor structure (Guay, Morin, Litalien, Valois, & Vallerand, 2015). ESEM was also used to examine predictive validity using path analysis to compare discovered latent factors' relationship with children's spring math and reading scores using a single framework that reduces measurement error and inflated correlations (Marsh, Morin, Parker, & Kaur, 2014). To determine the number of factors, preliminary analysis included Horn's (1965) parallel analysis and Velicer's (1976) minimum average partial (MAP) test. The optimal factor solution was chosen by comparing the Akaike Information Criterion (AIC) and Adjusted Bayesian Information Criterion (adjusted BIC) for the nonnested ESEM models (Kline, 2005). After determining the optimal factor solution the following fix indices were used to determine model fit: Comparative Fit Index (CFI), Tucker and Lewis Index (TLI), and Root Mean Square of Approximation fit index (RMSEA) (Fabrigar et al., 1999). Similar to previous research on national data sets, additional child and family demographic variables were included in the models: gender (males, females), race (minority, White), lunch fees (free/reduced lunch fee, paid lunch), preschool attendance (attended preschool, did not attend preschool) and kindergarten children's fall and spring math and reading scores.

There were missing data (about 2%); therefore, using the statistical package R version 3.3.3, we ran a test of data missing completely at random (MCAR). It was significant, $p < .00001$, indicating that the data were not missing completely at random. Data were determined to be missing at random; therefore, a random forest data imputation was performed for the missing values. Data were not imputed for missing covariates such as gender, race, lunch status or preschool attendance and data were missing at random. Three students were missing gender, race, and lunch status; therefore, those students were not included in the analysis. The final sample consisted of 472 kindergarten students (see Table 1).

An assumption of ESEM is that data are multivariate normal; therefore, normality, linearity, equality of variances, and multicollinearity of the data were examined. The assumptions of linearity and equality of variances were met. The assumption of multicollinearity was also met with all tolerances for the predictor variables above .10 and all VIFs were below 10. Using Mardia's test of multivariate normality, the data were found to be multivariate non-normal. Additionally, data were examined for pre-existing differences between the covariates. All models included a cluster component to control for the effect of teachers on students' ratings.

Table 1
Essential Skills Kindergarten Readiness Demographics

	N	Mean	SD	Skewness	Kurtosis
All students	472	2.976	0.685	-0.381	-0.600
Males	254	2.920	0.703	-0.296	-0.746
Females	218	3.041	0.656	-0.470	-0.368
Minority Students	170	2.953	0.625	-0.191	-0.602
White Students	302	2.989	0.716	-0.463	-0.617
Students with Aid	375	2.885	0.668	-0.292	-0.531
Students without Aid	097	3.326	0.633	-0.996	0.154
Students with Preschool	253	3.090	0.634	-0.438	-0.447
Students w/o Preschool	154	2.760	0.717	-0.055	-0.799

Construct validity

The data analysis was conducted using the Statistical Package Mplus version 7.11 to perform an ESEM (Exploratory Structural Equation Model), using MLR (robust maximum likelihood estimator), that is robust to the violation of multivariate normality (Marsh, Liem, Martin, Morin, & Nagengast, 2011). The model included multilevel data; therefore, it was most appropriate to use a complex sampling estimator to estimate the standard errors. The rotation used was the default, Geomin. The Geomin rotation is recommended when little is known about the loading structure (Asparouhov & Muthen, 2009). Three-factor, four-factor and five-factor ESEM solutions results were compared.

The three ESEM models were not nested; therefore, the AIC and BIC adjusted were used to determine the best model fit. The results of the models' AIC and the adjusted BIC suggested a five-factor solution, thus supporting the MAP results (see Table 2).

Table 2
Goodness of Fit Indexes for the Three-, Four-, and Five-Factor Models

Model	AIC	ADJ BIC	χ^2	df	CFI	TLI	RMSEA [90% CI]
3 Factor ESEM	25562.909	25675.723	1564.226*	365	0.816	0.773	0.090 [0.085, 0.094]
4 Factor ESEM	25244.963	25376.162	1587.660*	343	0.809	0.749	0.094 [0.090, 0.099]
5 Factor ESEM	25018.548	25167.296	1357.191*	322	0.868	0.816	0.089 [0.084, 0.094]

The AIC and the adjusted BIC for the five-factor solution were smaller than the four-factor and three-factor solutions AIC and adjusted BIC. To determine the factors, the factor loadings of the five-factor solution were examined using the 0.30 threshold and the hypothesis test for the factor loadings. Items that yield significant hypothesis tests but were below the 0.30 threshold were not considered important items for that factor. Additionally, items that were above the 0.30 threshold, but the hypothesis test were not significant were also not considered important items for that factor (see Table 3). An item that cross-loaded on more than one factor was considered important for all factors for which it loaded, if it was above the .30 threshold and the hypothesis test was significant.

For the ESEM model, there are R^2 values for each item, much like communalities in an exploratory factor analysis. These values suggest an adequate amount of variance explained with R^2 values ranging from .41 to .84 (see Table 3), but also indicated item cross-loadings. Similar to communalities, R^2 values above .70 indicate high overlap among items and the potential for cross loadings, providing additional support for the use of an ESEM model versus a CFA. An advantage of using an ESEM analysis is that it allows for crossing loadings among the variables (Guay et al., 2015; Marsh et al., 2011; Marsh et al., 2014). Based on our listed criteria for determining important factor loadings, four of the 23 items cross-loaded on more than one factor. The five dimensions of kindergarten readiness theoretically overlap and are interrelated; therefore, these findings are coherent with the underlying theory of kindergarten readiness. The results for the five-factor solution suggested the following factors: Factor 1 as approaches toward learning; Factor 2 as cognition and general knowledge; Factor 3 as language; Factor 4 as social and emotional; and Factor 5 as literacy. Using an ESEM analysis provides the advantages of examining model fit statistics for an EFA model. For good model fit, CFI and TLI values greater than 0.90 and 0.95 reflect adequate and excellent fit, respectively; RMSEA values below 0.08 and 0.05 reflect adequate fit and close fit (Marsh et al., 2011).

Table 3
Five-Factor Model Factor Loadings and R^2 (Communalities) for Each Item

Item	Dimension	Factor 1 ATL Loadings	R^2	Factor 2 CGK Loadings	R^2	Factor 3 Language Loadings	R^2	Factor 4 S&E Loadings	R^2	Factor 5 Literacy Loadings	R^2
1	ATL	0.86	0.79								
2	ATL	0.94	0.87								
3	ATL	0.81	0.82								
4	CGK			0.53	0.56						
5	CGK			0.95	0.83						
6	CGK			0.72	0.73						
7	L&L					0.86	0.82				
8	L&L					0.80	0.82				
9	L&L	0.60	0.74								
10	L&L	0.70	0.74								
11	L&L			0.39	0.41						
12	L&L	0.34	0.57	0.40	0.57			-0.15*			
13	L&L	0.43	0.63					-0.17*		0.38	0.63
14	L&L									0.67	0.65
15	L&L									0.85	0.82
16	L&L									0.67	0.65
17	P&M			0.57	0.68			0.40	0.68		
18	P&M			0.31ns				0.63	0.70		
19	S&E							0.67	0.78		
20	S&E	0.41	0.84					0.61	0.84		
21	S&E	0.39	0.84					0.64	0.84		
22	S&E							0.80	0.80		
23	S&E							0.89	0.84		

Note. All factor loadings, except one, presented were significant, $p < .05$; however, an asterisk indicates that the factor loading was less than 0.3. Item 18's factor loading for factor 2 was .31, but was not significant. The dimensions are labeled using the following abbreviations: Approaches toward learning (ATL), Cognition/General Knowledge (CGK), Language and Literacy (L&L), Physical and Motor (P&M), and Social and Emotional (S&E).

The CFI for the model is .841; TLI is .778; and RMSEA is .089. Overall, the five-factor model does not appear to be a good fit of the data.

Concurrent validity

To examine concurrent validity, the five-factor and one-factor ESEM models were analyzed (see Table 4) and both models included the covariates: gender, race, lunch aid status, and preschool experience. In the five-factor model, Factor 5 or literacy predicted fall reading scores (standardized coefficient = 0.778) and fall math scores (standardized coefficient = 0.537). Children's fall reading and math scores accounted for a moderate amount of the variance for the five-factor model, $R^2 = 0.56$ and $R^2 = 0.51$, respectively. The one-factor model—overall school readiness score—predicted fall reading scores (standardized coefficient = 0.317) and fall math scores (standardized coefficient = 0.416). Children's fall reading and math scores accounted for a small amount of the variance for the one-factor model, $R^2 = 0.23$ and $R^2 = 0.29$, respectively.

Table 4
Direct Effects of the Five-Factor and the Overall School Readiness Factor on the Fall Math and Fall Reading Scores

	Coefficient	Standard Error	p
Factor 5 (Literacy) →Reading	0.778	0.095	0.000*
Factor 5 (Literacy) →Math	0.537	0.098	0.000*
Factor 1 School Readiness →Reading	0.317	0.076	0.000*
Factor 1 School Readiness →Math	0.416	0.061	0.000*

Predictive validity

The ESEM five-factor model included path analysis examining direct effects for each of the discovered factors and children's spring math and reading scores. Gender, minority status, lunch aid status, preschool experience, and children's fall reading and math scores were included in the model. Based on the results, none of the readiness factors predicted spring reading scores (see Table 5). However, three of the six covariates predicted children's spring reading scores: gender, fall reading scores, and fall math scores.

Table 5
Direct Effects of the Five Latent Factors, Covariates and Fall Reading Scores Based on the Five-Factor Model for Spring Reading Scores

	Coefficient	Standard Error	p
Factor 1 →Reading: Approaches toward Learning	0.032	0.069	0.641
Factor 2 →Reading: Cognition and General Knowledge	0.032	0.082	0.696
Factor 3 →Reading: Language	0.074	0.091	0.420
Factor 4 →Reading: Social and Emotional	0.060	0.052	0.254
Factor 5 →Reading: Literacy	-0.138	0.095	0.146
Male →Reading	-0.106	0.037	0.016*
Minority →Reading	-0.028	0.036	0.527
Aid Recipient →Reading	0.001	0.035	0.989
Preschool Experience →Reading	-0.059	0.032	0.122
Fall reading →Reading	0.271	0.058	0.001*
Fall math →Reading	0.482	0.056	0.000*

There was also a negative relationship between gender and children's spring reading scores. Males' reading scores in the spring were significantly lower than females' reading scores in the spring (standardized coefficient = -0.106). Finally, children's fall math scores predicted children's spring reading scores (standardized coefficient = 0.482). The predictors in the five-factor reading model accounted for 51% of the variance in the spring reading scores, $R^2 = 0.51$. There were similar results in the model with children's spring math scores for the discovered factors (see Table 6). None of the discovered factors were significantly related to children's spring math scores. Additionally, only children's fall math scores predicted children's spring math scores (standardized coefficient = 0.633). The predictors in the five-factor math model accounted for 44% of the variance in the spring reading scores, $R^2 = 0.44$.

Adding the direct assessments of the kindergartners' fall math and reading scores could have overcontrolled the data, leaving little variance for the factors to explain children's reading and math scores in the spring. This limitation was examined with a post hoc

Table 6
Direct Effects of the Five Latent Factors, Covariates and Fall Math Based on the Five-Factor Model for Spring Math Scores

	Coefficient	Standard Error	p
Factor 1 →Math: Approaches toward Learning	0.041	0.072	0.565
Factor 2 →Math: Cognition and General Knowledge	-0.013	0.063	0.842
Factor 3 →Math: Language	0.040	0.086	0.642
Factor 4 →Math: Social and Emotional	0.055	0.072	0.444
Factor 5 →Math: Literacy	0.047	0.119	0.696
Male →Math	0.004	0.045	0.930
Minority →Math	0.082	0.052	0.118
Aid Recipient →Math	-0.001	0.034	0.987
Preschool Experience →Math	-0.067	0.035	0.054
Fall reading →Math	0.022	0.070	0.748
Fall math →Math	0.633	0.077	0.000*

Table 7
Direct Effects of the Five Latent Factors on the Spring Reading and Math Scores Based on Partially Controlled Five-Factor Model

	Coefficient	Standard Error	p
Factor 1 →Reading: Approaches toward Learning	0.144	0.125	0.250
Factor 2 →Reading: Cognition and General Knowledge	-0.034	0.160	0.832
Factor 3 →Reading: Language	0.052	0.136	0.701
Factor 4 →Reading: Social and Emotional	-0.013	0.079	0.864
Factor 5 →Reading: Literacy	0.337	0.141	0.017*
Factor 1 →Math: Approaches toward Learning	0.177	0.111	0.078
Factor 2 →Math: Cognition and General Knowledge	0.006	0.138	0.964
Factor 3 →Math: Language	0.025	0.117	0.710
Factor 4 →Math: Social and Emotional	-0.031	0.106	0.702
Factor 5 →Math: Literacy	0.401	0.140	0.000*

Note. Partially controlled model excludes children's beginning math and reading scores as controls.

ESEM model that excluded children's fall math and reading scores (see Table 7). The results of the post hoc ESEM path analysis for the discovered factors and the spring reading and math scores were different than the ESEM fully-controlled model. Factor 5, literacy, predicted children's spring reading (standardized coefficient = 0.337) and spring math scores (standardized coefficient = 0.401).

Reliability

Using the statistical package R version 3.3.3, internal consistency of reliability of the ESKRA was examined using the Cronbach's alpha and McDonald's omega (see Table 8). The Cronbach's alpha reliability coefficient is 0.96 with a 95% confidence interval from 0.951 to 0.962. The McDonald's omega reliability coefficient for the overall scale was 0.96 with a 95% confidence interval from 0.949 to 0.962. The omega reliability coefficient for five-factors was 0.977, and the discovered factors McDonald's omega reliability coefficients range from 0.87 to 0.95. Based on the results, the ESKRA has high internal consistency for the overall scale and all five discovered factors.

Table 8
Reliability Coefficients for Each of the Discovered Factors

Essential Skills	alpha	CI lower	CI upper	Omega	CI lower	CI upper
Factor 1: Approaches to learning	0.94	0.93	0.95	0.94	0.93	0.95
Factor 2: Cognition	0.90	0.88	0.92	0.89	0.87	0.91
Factor 3: Language	0.89	0.87	0.91	0.90	0.87	0.92
Factor 4: Social and Emotional	0.94	0.94	0.95	0.95	0.94	0.96
Factor 5: Literacy	0.87	0.85	0.89	0.87	0.85	0.89

Discussion

Although we expected the five-factor model for our data would align with the NEGP's five dimensions of kindergarten readiness, only four of the five factors' themes aligned with this theoretical framework: approaches toward learning; social and emotional; language and literacy; and cognition and general knowledge dimensions. In the current study, items related to physical well-being and motor skills did not form a separate factor. One potential explanation is that there were only two items for this dimension and both items addressed kindergartners' gross motor skills (i.e., attends to daily needs and follows basic health and safety rules). A factor should contain three or more items and is better defined the more items it contains (Marsh, Lüdtke, Nagengast, Morin, & Von Davier, 2103). The two items both loaded on the social and emotional factor. Because the two items are centered on children being able to take care of themselves, teachers may have viewed these two items as closely related to self-care skills that are often associated with social and emotional skills.

Another deviation from the expected five-factor model proposed by the NEGP was that the items related to language split into two separate factors: one factor related to language skills and a separate factor related to literacy skills. However, Factor 3—language—only had two items, which is lower than the recommended three or more items to claim a well-defined factor (Marsh et al., 2013). The discovered literacy factor, however, seemed to be important for establishing concurrent validity. The literacy factor within the discovered five-factor model, separate from the language factor, predicted kindergartners' fall reading and math scores, demonstrating concurrent validity for this subscale. It should be noted, however, that only the literacy factor, and not the other four factors, predicted fall reading and math scores. For this first analysis of the ESKRA, we wondered if the inclusion of direct assessments of kindergartners' fall math and reading scores might have severely limited the variance available for the factors to explain children's reading and math scores in the spring. In a post hoc ESEM path analysis removing the fall reading and math scores, Factor 5—literacy—predicted children's reading scores in the spring and children's math scores in the spring. These findings are consistent with previous research that has reported that direct assessments of kindergarten children's reading skills were consistently associated with reading and math achievement scores in later grades (Duncan et al., 2007; Grissmer et al., 2010; Hooper et al., 2010; Pagani et al., 2010; Romano et al., 2010). Yet, previous research has also revealed that approaches to learning and cognition consistently predicted children's later reading and math outcomes (Duncan et al., 2007; Grissmer et al., 2010). In the current study, our results did not find that the children's scores on the approaches to learning factor and cognition factor predicted children's spring reading and math scores.

Despite the lack of predictive validity evidence for all five factors, reliability coefficients for each of the discovered factors were high. Although these high values may indicate item redundancy (Streiner, 2003), reliability for the individual factors were in the appropriate range, indicating low measurement error. Based on the overall internal consistency for this brief assessment and the reliability for each of the factors, we have determined that this instrument is reliable.

Although the reliability for the factors was appropriate, limitations in the methods and data analysis might have contributed to less optimal findings related to validity. First, the ESKRA only included 23-items across five dimensions, with only two items for the subscale for physical development. At least three to five items are recommended for ESEM (Fabrigar et al., 1999). Moreover, although we included demographic variables about children and families in the model, no information about the teacher was included in the model. The data are nested; therefore, the model did include a cluster component to control for the effects of teachers revealing that teachers do influence readiness ratings. However, we were not able to determine the specific impact that teachers have on students' ratings using the cluster approach. Currently, the hierarchical approach is not available for the ESEM analysis. Research has demonstrated that teachers have implicit biases about race, gender, and socioeconomic status that impact how they treat and judge the academic abilities of students (Tenenbaum & Ruck, 2007). Future investigations of this assessment must take into account additional information about teachers.

In conclusion, the statistical results did not provide strong evidence of construct or predictive validity for the ESKRA. Using child and family control variables, none of the five discovered factors predicted children's spring math or reading outcomes, and even with pretest controls removed, the overall school readiness factor explained little variance for children's spring math and reading scores. However, kindergarten readiness has been described as children's being "ready to learn." Future research should consider examining growth in reading and math scores from fall to spring as a dependent measure to examine the predictive validity of this assessment.

Although teachers can provide valuable insight into the skills that can help children succeed in school, additional items that predicted children's math and reading outcomes in previous research should be included (Duncan et al., 2007; Grissmer et al., 2010; Hooper et al., 2010; Pagani et al., 2010; Romano et al., 2010). Once additional items have been added, the instrument should be re-examined using an ESEM for construct and predictive validity. After several iterations of this process, a more valid and reliable instrument that can help identify children who are not ready for kindergarten can be established.

Currently, there is no national instrument that assesses kindergarten readiness. Like most communities, this local school district developed its own assessment tool to examine their community wide efforts to increase children's kindergarten readiness. Continued modifications to the items in the ESKRA and hierarchical model testing may strengthen the predictive power of the instrument. This research is important to provide communities with information that will help shape community services and initiatives for children and families to help prepare young students to get ready to learn. Policymakers in local governments and/or non-profit community agencies can use community-level data to focus on certain school readiness dimensions, increasing program effectiveness with the community.

References

Asparouhov, T. & Muthén, B. (2009). Exploratory structural equation modeling. *Structural Equation Modeling, 16,* 397–438. doi: 10.1080/10705510903008204

Bierman, K. L., Domitrovich, C. E., Nix, R. L., Welsh, J. A., & Gest, S. D. (2008). Promoting academic and social-emotional school readiness: The Head Start REDI program. *Child Development, 79*(6), 1802–1817. doi:10.1111/j.1467-8624.2008.01227.x

Blair, C. (2001). The early identification of risk for grade retention among African American children at risk for school difficulty. *Applied Developmental Science, 5*(1), 37–50. doi:10.1207/S1532480XADS0501_4

Blair, C., & Razza, R. P. (2007). Relating effortful control, executive function, and false belief understanding to emerging math and literacy ability in kindergarten. *Child Development, 78*(2), 647–663. doi:10.1111/j.1467-8624.2007.01019.x

Cameron, C. E., Murrah, W. M., Grissmer, D., Brock, L. L., Bell, L. H., Worzalla, S. L., & Morrison, F. J. (2012). Fine motor skills and executive function both contribute to kindergarten achievement. *Child Development, 83*(4), 1229–1244. doi:10.1111/j.1467-8624.2012.01768.x

Carney, A. G., & Merrell, K. W. (2002). Reliability and comparability of a Spanish-language form of the preschool and kindergarten behavior scales. *Psychology in the Schools, 39*(4), 367–373. doi:10.1002/pits.10033

Child Trends. (2001, October). School readiness: Helping communities get children ready for school and schools ready for children (Research brief). Washington, DC: Child Trends. Retrieved from http://www.childtrends.org/wp-content/uploads/2013/03/schoolreadiness.pdf

Conn-Powers, M. (2008). Critical skills for children entering kindergarten: Essential skills for successful school readiness. Retrieved from Indiana University, Indiana Institute on Disability & Communication website: http://www.iidc.indiana.edu/styles/iidc/ defiles/ECC/SRSkills%20for%20Shared%20Expectations.pdf

Duncan, G. J., & Rafter, E. M. (2005). Concurrent and predictive validity of the Phelps kindergarten readiness scale II. *Psychology in the Schools, 42*(4), 355–359. doi:10.1002/pits.20096

Fabrigar, L. R., Wegener, D. T., MacCallum, R. C., & Strahan, E. J. (1999). Evaluating the use of exploratory factor analysis in psychological research. *Psychological Methods, 4*(3), 272–299. doi:10.1037/1082-989X.4.3.272

Forry, N. & Wessel, J. (2012, November). *Defining school readiness in Maryland: A multi-dimensional perspective* (Report No. 2012-44). Washington, DC: Child Trends.

Graue, M. E. (1993). *Ready for what? Constructing meanings of readiness for kindergarten*. Albany, NY: State University of New York Press.

Gredler, G. R. (1992). *School readiness: Assessment and educational issues*. Brandon, VT: Clinical Publishing. Retrieved from http://files.eric.ed.gov/fulltext/ED375979.pdf

Grimm, K. J., Steele, J. S., Mashburn, A. J., Burchinal, M., & Pianta, R. C. (2010). Early behavioral associations of achievement trajectories. *Developmental Psychology, 46*(5), 976–983. doi:10.1037/a0018878

Grissmer, D., Grimm, K. J., Aiyer, S. M., Murrah, W. M., & Steele, J. S. (2010). Fine motor skills and early comprehension of the world: Two new school readiness indicators. *Developmental Psychology, 46*(5), 1008–1017. doi:10.1037/a0020104

Guay, F., Morin, A., Litalien, D., Valois, P., & Vallerand, R. J. (2015). Application of exploratory structural equation modeling to evaluate the Academic Motivation Scale. *Journal of Experimental Education, 83*(1), 51–82.

Gullo, D. F. (2015). Assessment and school readiness: Implications for children, implications for schools. In O. N. Saracho (Eds.), *Contemporary perspectives on research in assessment and evaluation in early childhood education* (pp. 43–67). Charlotte, NC: IAP Information Age Publishing.

Heckman, J. J. (2006). Skill formation and the economics of investing in disadvantaged children. *Science, 312*(5782), 1900–1902. doi:10.1126/science.1128898

Hooper, S. R., Roberts, J., Sideris, J., Burchinal, M., & Zeisel, S. (2010). Longitudinal predictors of reading and math trajectories through middle school for African American versus Caucasian students across two samples. *Developmental Psychology, 46*(5), 1018–1029. doi:10.1037/a0018877

Horn, J. L., (1965). A rationale and test for the number of factors in factor analysis. *Psychometrika, 30*(2), 179–185.

Kagan, S. L, Moore, E., & Bradekamp, S. (1995). *Reconsidering children's early development and learning: Toward common views and vocabulary* (Report No. ISBN-0-16-048151-1). Washington, DC: National Education Goals Panel Goal 1 Technical Planning Group. Retrieved from http://files.eric.ed.gov/fulltext/ED391576.pdf

Kagan, S. L., & Rigby, E. (2003). *Policy matters: Setting and measuring benchmarks for state policies*. Washington, DC: Center for the Study of Social Policy. Retrieved from http://www.cssp.org/publications/public-policy/policy-matters-improving-the-readiness-of-children-for-school.pdf

Kline, R. B. (2005). *Methodology in the social sciences. Principles and practice of structural equation modeling (2nd ed.)*. New York, NY: Guilford Press.

Kurdek, L. A., & Sinclair, R. J. (2001). Predicting reading and mathematics achievement in fourth-grade children from kindergarten readiness scores. Journal of Educational *Psychology, 93*(3), 451–455. doi:10.1037/0022-0663.93.3.451

Ladd, G. W., Buhs, E., & Seid, M. (2000). Children's initial sentiments about kindergarten: Is school liking an antecedent of early classroom participation and achievement? *Merrill-Palmer Quarterly, 46,* 255–279 Retrieved from http://www.jstor.org/stable/ 23093716?seq=1#page_scan_tab_contents

Lloyd, J. E., & Hertzman, C. (2009). From kindergarten readiness to fourth-grade assessment: Longitudinal analysis with linked population data. *Social Science & Medicine, 68*(1), 111. doi:10.1080/01443410903165391

Lonigan, C. J., Phillips, B. M., Clancy, J.L., Landry, S. H., Swank, P. R., Assel, M., ... & The School Readiness Consortium. (2015). Impacts of a comprehensive School Readiness curriculum for Preschool children at risk for educational difficulties. *Child Development, 86*(6), 1773–1793. doi:10.1111/cdev.12460

Marsh, H. W., Liem, G. A., Martin, A. J., Morin, A., & Nagengast, B. (2011). Methodological measurement fruitfulness of exploratory structural equation modeling (ESEM): New approaches to key substantive issues in motivation and engagement. *Journal of Psychoeducational Assessment, 29*(4), 322–346.

Marsh, H. W., Lüdtke, O., Nagengast, B., Morin, A., & Von Davier, M. (2013). Why item parcels are (almost) never appropriate: Two wrongs do not make a right— Camouflaging misspecification with item parcels in CFA models. *Psychological Methods, 18*(3), 257–284. doi: 10.1037/a0032773

Marsh, H. W., Morin, A., Parker, P. D., & Kaur, G. (2014). Exploratory structural equation modeling: An integration of the best features of exploratory and confirmatory factor analysis. *Annual Review of Clinical Psychology, 10,* 58–110. doi: 10.1146/annurev-clinpsy-032813-153700

Meisels, S. J., Henderson, L. W., Liaw, F., Browning, K., & Have, T. T. (1993). New evidence for the effectiveness of the early screening inventory. *Early Childhood Research Quarterly, 8*(3), 327–346. doi:10.1016/S0885-2006(05)80071-7

National Association for the Education of Young Children & National Association of Early Childhood Specialists in State Departments of Education (2003). *Early childhood curriculum, assessment, and program evaluation: Position statement.* Retrieved from: https://www.naeyc.org/sites/default/files/globally-shared/downloads/PDFs/resources/position-statements/pscape.pdf

Pagani, L. S., & Fitzpatrick, C. (2014). Children's school readiness: Implications for eliminating future disparities in health and education. *Health Education & Behavior, 41*(1), 25–33. doi:10.1177/1090198113478818

Pagani, L. S., Fitzpatrick, C., Archambault, I., & Janosz, M. (2010). School readiness and later achievement: A French Canadian replication and extension. *Developmental Psychology, 46*(5), 984–994. doi:10.1037/a0018881

Quirk, M., Mayworm, A., Edyburn, K., & Furlong, M. J. (2016). Dimensionality and measurement invariance of a school readiness screener by ethnicity and home language. *Psychology in the Schools, 53*(7), 772–784. doi:10.1002/pits.21935

Romano, E., Babchishin, L., Pagani, L. S., & Kohen, D. (2010). School readiness and later achievement: Replication and extension using a nationwide Canadian survey. *Developmental Psychology, 46*(5), 995–1007. doi:10.1037/a0018880

Scott-Little, C., Kagan, S. L., & Frelow, V. S. (2006). Conceptualization of readiness and the content of learning: The intersection of policy and research. *Early Childhood Research Quarterly, 21,* 153–173.

Sijtsma, K. (2009). On the use, the misuse, and the very limited usefulness of Cronbach's alpha. *Psychometrika, 74*(1), 107–120. doi:10.1007/s11336-008-9101-0

Snow, K. L. (2006). Measuring school readiness: Conceptual and practical considerations. *Early Education and Development, 17*(1), 7–41. doi:10.1207/s15566935eed1701_2

Snow, C. E. & Van Hemel, S. B (Eds.). (2008). *Early childhood assessment: Why, what, and how?* Retrieved from The National Research Council of the National Academies website:https://www.acf.hhs.gov/sites/default/files/opre/early_child_assess.pdf

Streiner, D. L. (2003). Starting at the beginning: An introduction to coefficient alpha and internal consistency. *Journal of Personality Assessment, 80,* 99–103. doi:10.1207/S15327752JPA8001_18

Tenenbaum, H. R., & Ruck, M. D. (2007). Are teachers' expectations different for racial minority than European American students? A meta-analysis. *Journal of Educational Psychology, 99*(2), 253–273.

Texas Early Learning Council (2011, September). *Defining school readiness: National trends in school readiness definitions.* Retrieved from http://earlylearningtexas.org/media/10138/ trends%20in%20school%20readiness%20final%2011-1.pdf

Tramontana, M. G., Hooper, S. R., & Selzer, S. C. (1988). Research on the preschool prediction of later academic achievement: A review. *Developmental Review, 8*(2), 89–146.

U.S. Department of Education. (2015, April). *Matter of equality: Preschool in America.* Retrieved from https://www2.ed.gov/documents/early-learning/matter-equity-preschool-america.pdf

Velicer, W. F. (1976). Determining the number of components from the matrix of partial correlations. *Psychometrika, 41*(3), 321–327.

Wakabayashi, T., & Beal, J. A. (2015). Assessing school readiness in early childhood: Historical analysis, current trends. In O. N. Saracho (Eds.), *Contemporary perspectives on research in assessment and evaluation in early childhood education* (pp. 69–91). Charlotte, NC: IAP Information Age Publishing.

Welsh, J. A., Nix, R. L., Blair, C., Bierman, K. L., & Nelson, K. E. (2010). The development of cognitive skills and gains in academic school readiness for children from low-income families. *Journal of Educational Psychology, 102*(1), 43–53. doi:10.1037/a0016738

Adult Perceptions of an Inclusive Playground Designed and Built Based on the Results of Prior Studies Examining "Dream" Playgrounds

Tina L. Stanton-Chapman and Eric L. Schmidt

Abstract

The current investigation is part of a larger study examining the social participation patterns of children playing on an inclusive playground. The inclusive playground was designed and built by collating the results of the authors' previous studies examining adult and child perceptions of playgrounds in their communities. An anonymous survey was used to obtain data from a sample of caregivers, extended family members, childcare providers, and teachers who visited the inclusive playground designed for children ages 6 months to 12 years. To be included in the survey, individuals had to have visited the inclusive playground at least one time since it opened. A total of 357 individuals (96%) responded to and completed the whole survey. Fifteen (4%) individuals responded to the survey but reported that they did not visit the playground at any point since it opened, and thus were unable to answer remaining survey questions. Results indicate survey participants believed the inclusive playground meets the needs of all children, helps build turn-taking skills in children, and would recommend the inclusive playground to other families. Survey participants also report that they typically spend over 45 minutes at the inclusive playground when they visit with their children or students. Overcrowding of the inclusive playground is also discussed as a common data theme. The results demonstrate that community input is not only important when designing and building playgrounds, but it contributes to the overall popularity and satisfaction with the final playground product. These results should be considered in future work and in the design of future playgrounds in a given community.

Keywords: inclusion, playgrounds, disability, perceptions

The World Health Organization (WHO) defines social participation as two or more individuals sharing an activity or being involved together in life situations (2001). It often includes involvement in communication, mobility, self-care, and interpersonal interactions (Shikako-Thomas, Bogossian, Lach, Shevell, & Majnemer, 2013). The social participation of individuals in recreational activities is often not considered (WHO, 2001). Age, gender, residential location (e.g., urban, rural, suburban), the presence of a disability, and socioeconomic status are variables influencing children's social participation in play (King, Shields, Imms, Black, & Ardern, 2013). Social participation in children with disabilities is negatively influenced by physical barriers within the environmental setting and social exclusion by peers (WHO, 2008).

Existing research has pinpointed personal and environmental barriers to social participation in children with disabilities. Personal barriers affecting the social participation of children with disabilities include motor skill, cognitive skill, and social-emotional skill delays (Browder & Cooper, 1994; Solish, Perry, & Minnes, 2010). Environmental barriers impacting social participation in children with disabilities include organizational policies and practices, discrimination, societal attitudes, and architectural barriers (Rimmer, 2005). Combined, these barriers lead to decreased physical activity and decreased social participation in children with disabilities when compared to similar-age children who are typically developing regardless of disability category (Carlon, Taylor, Dodd, & Shields, 2013; King et al., 2013; Shields, Dodd, & Abblitt, 2009). To make equal access to social participation a reality for children with disabilities, playground designers and manufacturers must take into consideration the wide range of abilities in children (e.g., physical, psychological, personal stamina, individual preferences) (Stanton-Chapman & Schmidt, 2018).

Ensuring that children with disabilities benefit fully from the myriad of social opportunities and play experiences available to them remains a substantial challenge for them and their families. One area of particular concern is the play equipment located on community playgrounds (Rimmer, 2005). Community playgrounds fall under two categories—*neighborhood* and *destination* playgrounds. A neighborhood playground is defined as a playground that is built in a residential community (Brown & Burger, 1984). Its purpose is to provide children with a place to play within walking distance of where they live. A destination playground is defined as a playground that is built in a place where playground patrons are expected to drive or take public transportation to in order to utilize the play space (Brown & Burger, 1984). The play area and equipment may be the same or vary at neighborhood and destination playgrounds, but both have been found to be troublesome for social participation for individuals with disabilities (Rimmer, 2005).

Studies examining caregivers and special education professionals' perceptions of currently available playground equipment on community playgrounds have been conducted in current years. Two studies examining caregiver perceptions of community playgrounds targeting toddlers and preschoolers (Stanton-Chapman & Schmidt, 2017a) and school-age children (Stanton-Chapman & Schmidt, in press) found that (a) children with disabilities could not socially participate with current playground offerings; (b) caregivers believed the currently available playground equipment was developmentally inappropriate for children with disabilities despite what playground manufacturers advocate in terms of equipment; and (c) caregivers dreamed of a fully inclusive playground that meets the needs of all children. Special education professionals indicated that children with sensory needs (e.g., children with autism, hearing impairments, or visual impairments) have different needs on a playground that are currently unmet (Stanton-Chapman & Schmidt, 2016b). They advocated for sensory equipment (e.g., musical instruments, tactile architectural panels) on future playground builds. Many playgrounds are designed and built with little input from community residents. Methods of collecting community input such as incorporating the Collaborative Strategies Cycle, a Council for Exceptional Children, Division of Early Childhood recommended practice for outdoor environments, is critical for playground builds (Stanton-Chapman & Schmidt, 2016a).

The current investigation is part of a larger study examining the social participation patterns of children playing on an inclusive playground. This inclusive playground was designed and built by collating the results of our previous studies (e.g., Stanton-Chapman & Schmidt, 2016b, 2017a, 2018, in press) to create a community playground environment that best meets the needs of all families. In this study, the results of six online survey questions from adult participants whose children played on the inclusive playground are examined. The following survey questions guided the study: (a) what zones of the inclusive playground are frequented by children of survey participants; (b) how many minutes, on average, do survey participants stay at the inclusive playground when they visit; (c) do survey participants believe the inclusive playground appeals to children of all abilities; (d) do survey participants believe the playground looks like a playground for children with disabilities; (e) do survey participants believe the inclusive playground meets their child's abilities and helps develop his or her relationships with peers; and (f) do survey participants recommend the inclusive playground to other families?

Method

An anonymous survey was used to obtain data from a sample of caregivers, extended family members, child care providers, and teachers who visited an inclusive playground designed for children ages 6 months to 12 years. To protect survey participants' anonymity, all responses were collapsed into a "Response Report" by question at the conclusion of the survey.

Participants

Individuals who visited a newly built inclusive playground in a Midwestern city were surveyed from January 2018 to April 2018. Any adult or child over the age of 16, who visited the playground at least one time from when the playground opened in October 2017, was invited to participate in the online survey. Invitations to participate in the online survey were done through social media outlets, a local story in the city and community newspapers, and flyers given to local child care centers and elementary schools. The invitations described the study as a research project examining their thoughts on the new inclusive playground.

Demographic information was collected from respondents. Information such as age, gender, number of children in the family or classroom, and role to the children was collected (see Table 1). A total of 357 (96%) individuals responded to and completed the whole survey. Fifteen (4%) individuals responded to the survey but reported that they did not visit the playground at any point since it opened, and thus, were unable to answer remaining survey questions. Although the total number of individuals who were aware of the survey but did not complete it is unknown, 403 individuals clicked on the survey link. Of the 403 individuals who clicked on the survey link, 357 individuals (88%) completed the entire online survey. Fifteen individuals (4%) opened the survey but were only able to answer question one without having visited the inclusive playground, and 31 individuals (7%) clicked on the survey link but did not answer any of the survey questions. Therefore, the overall response rate for the online survey is 372 individuals (92%) who answered one or more survey questions.

Setting Description for Survey

In fall 2017, a newly built inclusive playground opened to community residents in a large Midwestern metropolitan city. The results from the authors' prior studies (e.g., Stanton-Chapman & Schmidt, 2016b, 2017a, 2018, in press) were collated to inform the overall playground design. Specifically, the playground (a) focuses on varying disabilities including autism, hearing impairments, visual impairments, physical impairments, and intellectual disabilities; (b) is over 80% accessible to all individuals including those who require the use of mobility devices; (c) is developmentally appropriate for children ages 6 months to 12 years; and (d) allows grandparents and caregivers with disabilities (i.e., Wounded Warriors) who use mobility devices to be in close proximity to their children, as the majority of the facility is ground level. The authors' main goals for the playground were to design a playground that would meet the needs of children across varying abilities and ages, hold children's interest for a minimum of 30 minutes, and be designed in such a manner that it would not appear to be a playground for children with disabilities, but rather a playground for individuals of *all* abilities.

The playground is 11,000 square feet in size and has seven play zones (infant/toddler, musical instruments, sensory maze, hill structure, mega-tower, zipline, traditional swings, accelerator swing). A complete description of each play zone with color pictures can be found in Stanton-Chapman and Schmidt (2017b). Please refer to Figure 1 for an overview picture of the inclusive playground.

Figure 1. Visual of the inclusive playground.

Survey Measure

For the purpose of the study, a caregiver, extended family member, childcare provider, and teacher satisfaction survey (22 items) was developed. The survey gathered information on respondents' perceptions of the overall playground design and its equipment, and their perceptions of the playground for children with disabilities. The survey was anonymous and contained two types of questions: (a) close-ended questions, where respondents selected the most appropriate answer from a list of choices, and (b) open-ended questions. The total survey consisted of 22 questions. Fifteen of the questions were close-ended and focused on demographics and perceptions. These questions asked participants to select the most appropriate answer from a list of choices. Seven of the questions were open-ended questions where the respondents first selected the most appropriate answer from a list of choices (e.g., strongly agree, agree, neutral, disagree, strongly disagree) and then provided a written response for elaboration purposes. The current study reports on nine close-ended questions (e.g., demographics; preferences) and four open-ended questions. The open-ended questions were as follows: (a) The playground appeals to children of all abilities, (b) The playground looks like a playground for children with disabilities, (c) The playground meets my child's abilities and helps develop his or her relationships with peers, and (d) I would recommend the playground to other families. The respondents were expected to provide a brief narrative explaining their answer.

The survey utilized in the current study presents an overview of the results regarding the inclusive playground. The goal of the survey was to ascertain initial adult perceptions of the inclusive playground, specifically whether the playground met the needs of the community. The findings from this survey will guide future investigations and grant proposals (e.g., child perception studies, direct observation studies, more in-depth analyses of the survey described in the current study).

Procedures

Data were collected during a 3-month period. Invitations to participate in the online survey were done through social media outlets, a local story in the city and community newspapers, and flyers given to local child care centers and elementary schools. In order to complete the survey, participants must have visited the inclusive playground at least once. Survey participants were not compensated for their survey responses. Participants who selected to complete the online survey clicked on the link and were taken to an online electronic consent letter. The survey appeared after the participant agreed to do the study. Only one family member per household was permitted to complete the online survey. The survey took 5 to 12 minutes to complete, depending on the amount of time participants devoted to the open-ended questions.

Data Analysis

Online survey results were entered into Microsoft Excel. Frequency counts of responses were conducted using Microsoft Excel's summation function. Open-ended responses were also entered into a Microsoft Excel spreadsheet. The responses were coded by two research staff who were pursuing a Bachelor of Arts degree with a concentration in Early Childhood Education. Both were enrolled in their final year of the education program and were also serving as student teachers in public elementary schools. A qualitative methodology expert provided feedback on methodological issues during the analysis. Using a content analysis procedure, participant responses were coded at the word or phrase level to capture the perspective that respondents were describing. It was possible that one response contained multiple key ideas. For example, a response to the statement, "The inclusive playground looks like a playground for children with disabilities"—i.e., "I don't know enough about disabilities, but it looks like a playground for everyone"—was coded in two different categories: participants did not have enough knowledge about disabilities to adequately answer the question; the appeal of the playground for children with and without disabilities.

To develop initial categories, one research staff member randomly selected and reviewed 25% of participant answers (90 responses) for each open-ended question and noted key ideas that were represented in each of the responses. Then the two research staff members reviewed the remaining participant responses looking for similarities across participants to develop themes. Once themes were identified, the research staff members defined the themes using exemplars from the participant responses. Responses that represented discrete units of thought and answered the question were categorized by the theme they exemplified. Incomplete answers that did not answer the question posed were sorted into a miscellaneous category.

Research staff members then used these thematic categories to independently code all participant responses for each open-ended question. Seventy-two participant responses (20%) were double-coded for each open-ended question through random selection for reliability purposes, yielding an overall interrater reliability of 91%. Disagreements were resolved through discussion to achieve mutual consensus among the coders.

Results

A total of 357 surveys were completed. Table 1 reports demographic information for survey respondents and their children.

Responses to close-ended questions

The zones of the inclusive playground frequented by children of survey participants are reported in Table 2. For this question, participants were asked to indicate if any child in their family or class had visited a given zone within the inclusive playground. Survey participants could select more than one zone if it applied to his or her family or classroom.

Participants were asked how many minutes on average they stay at the inclusive playground when they visit the facility. Of the 357 participants, 212 participants (59%) indicated that they spent over 45 minutes at the inclusive playground. Fifty participants (14%) reported staying at the inclusive playground for 31-45 minutes. Only 95 participants (27%) said they were at the inclusive playground less than 30 minutes.

Responses to open-ended questions

When asked if the inclusive playground appeals to children of all abilities, 265 participants (74%) strongly agreed with the statement, 74 participants (20%) agreed with the statement, 18 participants (5%) were neutral to the statement, and two participants (1%) disagreed with the statement. No survey participants strongly disagreed with the statement. Written responses revealed three themes: (a) over-crowding of the playground due to its popularity; (b) additional ideas for playground design and equipment; and (c) the appeal of the inclusive playground to children with and without disabilities. The first and second themes were more general in that participants provided feedback on how the authors could alter the inclusive playground in the future to address its overall popularity within the community. For example, one participant said, "There needs to be a medium section for preschool children who are too old for the toddler area but too small for the mega-tower." Another participant said, "The playground is very crowded, and I recommend that the developers add-on to it to relieve some of the crowding." The third theme centered on the overall inclusivity of the playground. This was defined as a playground facility where all children, including those with disabilities, can come and play together. A participant noted, "The playground is built with disabled children in mind; however, other children don't seem to be aware." Another participant mentioned the inclusive playground's attraction to children with sensory needs: "I am grateful to have a playground for my child's sensory needs."

The next open-ended question asked participants to respond to the statement, "The inclusive playground looks like a playground for children with disabilities." Respondents generally disagreed with this statement: 12 participants (3%) strongly agreed to this statement, 32 participants (9%) agreed to this statement, 101 participants (28%) were neutral to this statement, 140 participants (40%) disagreed with this statement, and 72 participants (20%) strongly disagreed to this statement. When analyzing the written comments, two themes emerged: participants did not have enough knowledge about disabilities to adequately answer the question and the appeal of the playground for children with and without disabilities was evident. There were no comments that could be categorized into a theme that described the inclusive playground as a playground for children with disabilities only. Theme 1 is defined as a lack of knowledge in disabilities including disability categories and special education terminology. One participant commented, "I don't know enough about disabilities to answer this question." Another participant said, "I don't know anyone with a disability to know what a disabled playground should look like." Theme 2 is defined as comments that center on the inclusive playground being appropriate for all children. For example, one participant said, "It [the playground] offers a lot for disabilities, but these areas look similar to other areas. The kids won't have to feel different." A second participant added, "It looks like a playground for everyone." Another said, "While the playground serves children with disabilities well, it looks like a regular playground to me."

When asked to respond to the statement, "The inclusive playground meets my child's abilities and helps develop his or her relationships with peers," 233 participants (65%) strongly agreed to the statement, 97 participants (27%) agreed to the statement, 26 participants (7.5%) were neutral to the statement, and 1 participant (0.5%) disagreed to the statement. No participants strongly disagreed to the statement. One theme emerged from the comments made by participants—the equipment at the inclusive playground forces children to take turns. One participant reflected, "Only one child can use the zipline. This means other children have to wait their turn to use it." Another participant discussed how the popularity of the inclusive playground also requires children to wait their turn: "There are so many kids at this playground on warm, sunny days that they are forced to wait their turn to do something." A third participant added, "The playground is so busy that it offers many opportunities to take turns and share."

When asked if they would recommend the inclusive playground to other families, 311 participants (87%) strongly agreed with the statement, 31 participants (9%) agreed with the statement, 7 participants (2%) were neutral to the statement, 5 participants (1%) disagreed with the statement, and 3 participants (1%) strongly disagreed with the statement. One theme emerged from the answers—the inclusive playground is so unique that the participants highly recommended to it their friends. A participant noted, "I highly recommend it [the playground]. It's amazing! It is colorful, different, and exciting. No other park compares." Another participant added, "Of course I recommend it [the playground] to others! I would like to see many more playgrounds like X [added the name of the playground]." A third participant said, "We tell people about the playground all of the time. We were sad to see the last playground go, but this playground exceeds all expectations." Despite the fact that eight participants disagreed or strongly disagreed with the statement that they would recommend the inclusive playground to other families, they did not provide any negative feedback to support their stance.

Discussion

The findings of this study further our understanding on the social participation of children on an inclusive playground that was specifically designed with input from caregivers and special education professionals. Survey respondents tended to be white, non-Hispanic mothers who were 31–40 years of age and had two children in their family. Their children varied in age, but the majority were birth to 8 years old. Demographics of survey participants reflect the demographics of the community where the inclusive playground is located. All playground zones were frequented by the children of survey participants. The most popular playground zones were the turf hill, the mega-tower, and the sensory maze. The least popular playground zones were the accelerator swing, the traditional swings, and the musical instruments. When survey participants visited the inclusive playground, the majority indicated that they spent over 45 minutes at the facility. Identifying aspects of the playground environment (e.g., equipment, design) that support or discourage physical activity in children has been the focus of research in recent years (Ding, Sallis, Kerr, Lee, & Rosenbery, 2011). The results of such studies indicate that children are more likely to be more physically active when fixed playground equipment exists on a school or community playground (Farley, Meriweather, Baker, Rice, & Webber, 2008; Stanton-Chapman & Schmidt, 2018). These studies examined children's physical activity levels on preexisting playgrounds not necessarily built to address community needs. This study is unique in that the inclusive playground was designed and built to meet the needs of individuals who indicated what they desired in their dream community playground. The fact that survey respondents said they on average spend over 45 minutes at the inclusive playground when they visit demonstrates that this playground accomplished its intended purpose.

Caregivers and special education professionals often report challenges in locating playgrounds that accommodate the range of ages, abilities, and interests of *all* children (Jeanes & Magee, 2012; Stanton-Chapman & Schmidt, 2016b; Stanton-Chapman & Schmidt, 2017a; Stanton-Chapman & Schmidt, 2018). Prior research has found that modifying the playground environment with more interesting materials and equipment may lead to changes in play behaviors of children and encourages more active and cooperative play (Bundy et al., 2009). The findings from this study support this notion, and also, indicate that playground designers and manufacturers should direct their attention to multi-informants (e.g., caregivers, teachers, special education professionals, park directors) and children's abilities across a continuum when designing a playground. In the current study, 94% ($N = 339$) of survey participants either strongly agreed or agreed with the statement that the inclusive playground appeals to children of *all* abilities. In earlier studies investigating if currently available playgrounds were developmentally appropriate for *all* children, 99% of special education professionals (Stanton-Chapman & Schmidt, 2016b), 65% of caregivers with children under the age of 5 years, and 65% of caregivers with children ages 5–12 years indicated that the majority of playgrounds were developmentally inappropriate. Given that the majority of survey participants either strongly agreed or agreed that the inclusive playgrounds meet the needs of all children and would recommend the inclusive playground to other families, future studies should continue to explore the use of the Collaborative Strategies Cycle when building future playgrounds (Stanton-Chapman & Schmidt, 2017b).

Written responses to many of the open-ended questions highlighted the overcrowding of the inclusive playground due to its popularity. The fact that the inclusive playground continues to have large crowds beyond its initial grand opening and during colder months is a finding that needs to be explored further. The effects of overcrowding on a playground have not been studied previously in the literature. It is possible that it could lead to bullying or aggression if not resolved. The overcrowding theme does reveal that the public will come to a community playground if it meets the needs of families and holds children's interest for an extended time period.

Limitations

This study has several limitations. First, this study involved heterogeneous groups of participants (e.g., mothers, fathers, grandparents, teachers) who volunteered to complete the survey after learning of it from social media, flyers, and newspaper stories. It is likely that survey participants tended to be those individuals who were more invested in the topic. Second, the sample only represents perspectives of adults in a specific geographic region (Midwest of the United States). Their perspectives of the inclusive playground may deviate from other individuals in varying states or countries. Third, it is possible that survey participants provided socially desirable answers especially, for the open-ended questions. The use of multisource and mixed-method strategies (e.g., interviews of adults and children; observations of children on the inclusive playground) would provide a more comprehensive dataset to assess the overall satisfaction of the inclusive playground. Fourth, to be included in the survey, individuals had to have visited the inclusive playground at least one time since it opened. Survey participants who did not visit the inclusive playground were prohibited from completing the remainder of the survey. It is possible, although highly unlikely, that individuals who did not visit the inclusive playground for at least one time answered "yes" to the first question and completed the remainder of the survey without our knowledge. It would be impossible to exclude their responses if this event occurred. As with any survey, we hope that the participants in the current study were truthful in their responses.

Implications

The current study is the first to explore the effects of an inclusive playground that was designed and built based on prior work examining the preferences of multiple informants (e.g., caregivers, special education professionals, observations of children playing on playgrounds). The results demonstrate that community input is not only important when designing and building playgrounds, but it contributes to the overall popularity and satisfaction with the final playground product. These results should be considered in future work and in the design of future playgrounds in a given community and is currently a recommended practice of the Council for Exceptional Children, Division of Early Childhood (Stanton-Chapman & Schmidt, 2016a). Given that overcrowding was a theme in the current study, future investigations should explore adult and child perceptions of the overcrowding and its effects on child behavior while playing.

Table 1
Demographic Information for Survey Respondents and Their Children (N = 357)

Demographics	Number of Participants	Percentage of Participants
Gender		
Male	61	17%
Female	293	82.5%
Prefer not to answer	3	0.5%
Relationship to Children		
Mother	204	57%
Father	58	16%
Grandparent	55	15%
Foster Parent	18	5%
Sister or Brother	1	1%
Aunt or Uncle	3	1%
Neighbor	1	1%
Teacher or child care provider	12	3%
Nanny	5	1%
Racial and Ethnic Category		
White, Non-Hispanic	300	84%
Black, African-American	22	7%
Hispanic or Latino	12	3%
Asian	5	1%
Two or more races or ethnicities	10	3%
Other	0	0%
Prefer not to answer	8	2%
Age		
20 years or younger	1	0.5%
21-30 years	37	10%
31-40 years	191	54%
41-50 years	72	20%
51-60 years	10	3%
61-70 years	45	12%
Over 71 years	1	0.5%
Number of children in family/class		
0 children	5	1%
1 child	56	16%
2 children	188	53%
3 or more children	108	30%

Table 1 Continued
Demographic Information for Survey Respondents and Their Children (N = 357)

Demographics	Number of Participants	Percentage of Participants
Child with a disability in family/class		
Yes	44	12%
No	313	88%
Age group of children in family/class		
Birth to 2 years	130	36%
3 to 4 years	178	50%
5 to 8 years	156	44%
8 to 12 years	71	20%
13 to 18 years	18	0.5%

Note. Participants could respond to multiple categories so not all percentages equal 100%.

Table 2
Zones of the Inclusive Playground Frequented by Children of Survey Participants

Playground Zones	Number of Participants	Percentage of Participants
Turf Hill	309	87%
Mega-Tower	293	82%
Sensory Maze	287	80%
Zipline	278	78%
Infant and Toddler	222	62%
Musical Instruments	212	59%
Traditional Swings	201	56%
Accelerator Swing	180	50%

Note. Participants could respond to multiple categories so not all percentages equal 100%.

Authors' Note

Correspondence should be sent to:
Tina L. Stanton-Chapman, Ph.D.
Early Childhood and Human Development
College of Education, Criminal Justice, and Human Services
University of Cincinnati
One Edwards Center
Cincinnati, OH 45221
Phone: 513-556-3600
E-mail: stantot@ucmail.uc.edu

Eric L. Schmidt, CPSI
Playground Equipment Services
8510 Coghill Lane
Cincinnati, OH 45239
Phone: 513-923-2333
E-mail: eric@playgroundequipmentservices.com

References

Browder, D. M., & Cooper, K. J. (1994). Inclusion of older adults with mental retardation in recreational activities. *Mental Retardation, 32*(2), 91–99.

Brown, J. G., & Burger, C. (1984). Playground designs and preschool children's behavior. *Environment and Behavior, 16*(5), 599–626.

Bundy, A. C., Luckett, T., Tranter, P. J., Naughton, G. l. A. Wyver, S., Ragen, J., Spies, G. (2009). "The risk is that there is no risk": A simple, innovative intervention to increase children's activity levels. *International Journal of Early Years Education, 17,* 33–45.

Carlon, S. L., Taylor, N. F., Dodd, K. J., & Shields, N. (2013). Differences in habitual activity levels of young people with cerebral palsy and their typically developing peers: A systematic review. *Disability and Rehabilitation, 35*(8), 647–655.

Ding, D., Sallis, J. F., Kerr, J., Lee, S., & Rosenberg, D. E. (2011). Neighborhood environment and physical activity among youth: A review. *American Journal of Preventative Medicine, 41*(4), 442–455.

Farley, T. A., Meriwether, R. A., Baker, E. T., Rice, J. C., & Webber, L. S. (2008). Where do the children play? The influence of playground equipment on physical activity of children in free play. *Journal of Physical Activity and Health, 5*(2), 319-331.

Jeanes, R., & Magee, J. (2012). Can we play on the swings and roundabouts?: Creating inclusive play spaces for disabled young people and their families. *Leisure Studies, 31*(2), 193–210. doi: 10.1080/02614367.2011

King, M., Shields, N., Imms, C., Black, M., & Ardern, C. (2013). Participation of children with intellectual disability compared with typically developing children. *Research in Developmental Disabilities, 34*, 1854–1862.

Rimmer, J. H. (2005). The conspicuous absence of people with disabilities in public fitness and recreational activities: Lack of interest or lack of access. *American Journal of Health Promotion, 19*(5), 327–329.

Shields, N., Dodd, K. J., & Abblitt, C. (2009). Do children with Down Syndrome perform sufficient physical activity to maintain good health?: A pilot study. *Adapted Physical Activity Quarterly, 26*, 307–320.

Shikako-Thomas, K, Bogossian, A., Lach, L., Shevell, M., & Majnemer, A. (2013). Parents' perspectives of the quality of life of adolescents with disabilities: Trajectory, choices and hope. *Disability and Rehabilitation, 35*(25), 2113–2122.

Solish, A., Perry, A., & Minnes, P. (2010). Participation of children with and without disabilities in social, recreational, and leisure activities. *Journal of Applied Research in Intellectual Disabilities, 23*, 226–236.

Stanton-Chapman, T. L., & Schmidt, E. L. (2016a). Creating inclusive playground environments following the Principles of Universal Design: Collaborative strategies to promote family participation in the design and development process. *Division of Early Childhood (DEC) in the Council for Exceptional Children (CEC) Monograph for Best Practices in Early Childhood Environments: Promoting meaningful access, participation, and inclusion* (pp. 87–100). (n.p.).

Stanton-Chapman, T. L., & Schmidt, E. L. (2016b). Special education professionals' attitudes towards accessible playgrounds and recreational facilities. *Research and Practice for Persons with Severe Disabilities, 41*(2), 90–100.

Stanton-Chapman, T. L., & Schmidt, E. L. (2017a). Caregiver perceptions of inclusive playgrounds targeting toddlers and preschoolers with disabilities: Has recent international and national policy improved overall satisfaction?" *Journal of Research in Special Educational Needs, 17*(4), 237–246.

Stanton-Chapman, T. L., & Schmidt, E. L. (2017b). Creating an inclusive playground for children of *all* abilities: West Fork Playground in Cincinnati, Ohio. *Children, Youth, and Environments, 27*(3), 124–137.

Stanton-Chapman, T. L., & Schmidt, E. L. (2018). An observational study of children's behaviors across two playgrounds: Similarities and differences. *Early Childhood Research Quarterly, 44*, 114–123.

Stanton-Chapman, T. L., & Schmidt, E. L. (in press). In search of equivalent social participation: What do caregivers of children with disabilities desire regarding inclusive recreational facilities and playgrounds? *Journal of International Special Needs Education.*

World Health Organization. (2001). *International Classification of Functioning, Disability, and Health (IFC).* Geneva: Author. http://apps.who.int/classifications/icfbrowser/.

World Health Organization. (2008). *Primary Health Care: Now More than Ever (IFC).* Geneva: Author. http://www.who.int/whr/2008/en/.

List of Contributors

Zeynep Biringen, Ph.D., is a developmental and clinical psychologist. She earned her master's degree at Stanford University and doctorate at the University of California at Berkeley. She did her MacArthur Postdoctoral training at the University of Colorado School of Medicine with Robert N. Emde and Inge Bretherton. Since 1996, she has been on the faculty of the Department of Human Development and Family Studies at Colorado State University and conducting basic science and intervention research focusing on emotional attachment and emotional availability (EA). She is also the President of emotionalavailability.com, LLC which is used for EA trainings. She discloses that she has a "conflict of interest" related to the use of the Emotional Availability (EA) Scales (which she developed) and, therefore, distanced herself from the main analyses of this study; she, however, has had no financial conflict of interest related to this project.

Patricia C. Clark is Professor of Early Childhood Education and Chair of the Department of Elementary Education at Ball State University. Dr. Clark's research focuses on teacher education, kindergarten readiness, and diversity issues. She works with communities on establishing early childhood coalitions that support young children and their families.

Shauna Skillern Fisher has an M.S. in Human Development and Family Studies. She is a Marriage and Family Therapist and Certified Additions Counselor. She maintains a private practice specializing in relationship issues, anxiety and trauma.

Kathryn L. Fletcher, Ph.D., is a professor of educational psychology at Ball State University where she teaches undergraduate and graduate courses in developmental psychology. Dr. Fletcher has expertise in child development and assessment and has published peer-reviewed research in the areas of early literacy and language development, school readiness, and the impact of parenting on academic achievement. She is also involved with numerous non-profit organizations to promote the optimal development of children and youth. Dr. Fletcher currently serves as an associate editor for *School Psychology*.

Randy G. Floyd, Ph.D., is a Professor of Psychology, Training Director for the School Psychology doctoral program, and Associate Chair in the Department of Psychology at The University of Memphis. His research focuses on understanding the measurement properties of psychological assessment techniques and professional publication practices in school psychology. Dr. Floyd has authored or coauthored more than 100 publications. He is a Fellow of the American Psychological Association Division 16 (School Psychology) and an elected member of the Society for the Study of School Psychology.

Annie C. Liner earned her Ph.D. in Educational Psychology from Ball State University. She worked for Head Start for a number of years igniting her passion for early literacy and kindergarten readiness. Dr. Liner is also an experienced college instructor currently teaching graduate research courses. She also spends time providing research and data consultation for graduate students completing their master thesis or doctoral dissertation.

Jennifer Gerber Moné, Ph.D., is a Licensed Marriage and Family Therapist in Denver, Colorado and maintains a successful private practice serving couples, individuals, and families. Her specialties include fertility concerns, grief and loss, including pregnancy loss, couples' relationships, divorce and high conflict, parenting, and life transitions. Dr. Moné' is an AAMFT Approved Supervisor for mental health professionals seeking licensure and is an EMDR-approved practitioner (EMDR is a therapeutic approach aimed at reducing the intensity of traumatic events and the thoughts and feelings associated with them).

Laura E. Murphy is a supervising psychologist at the Boling Center for Developmental Disabilities, a LEND institution where she has served as an educator and clinical researcher for 30 years. She has trained many psychology interns, fellows, interns, and graduate students in assessment and therapy. She has numerous national and international presentations at conferences and has a number of peer-reviewed publications. She is also a University of Tennessee Health Science Center Professor in the Department of Psychiatry. Her research interests include assessment and diagnosis of young children with neurodevelopmental disabilities and stress in families of young children with neurodevelopmental disabilities.

List of Contributors

Christine O'Brien is a graduate student in the School Psychology Psy.D. program at St. John's University, where she studies academic and behavioral functioning in children and adolescents. She earned her M.A. in psychology from Stony Brook University in 2016 and her B.A. in political science and public relations from Penn State University in 2011.

Eric L. Schmidt, CPSI, is the owner of Playground Equipment Equipment Services, a company that designs and builds playgrounds for schools and communities. Eric has been involved with 14 of the top 30 best inclusive playgrounds throughout the world. He is also the recipient of the 2018 Rising Star Award for the Colerain Chamber of Commerce in Cincinnati, Ohio.

Mark J. Sciutto is a Professor of Psychology at Muhlenberg College in Allentown, Pennsylvania. Dr. Sciutto's research focuses on the role that knowledge and misconceptions of Attention-Deficit/Hyperactivity Disorder (ADHD) might play in families' help-seeking behavior. He is also researching stigma related to ADHD and Autism Spectrum Disorders.

Kate Shepard, Ph.D., CCC-SLP, is a developmental psychologist and speech-language pathologist. She earned a B.S. in Human Development and Family Studies from Colorado State University, an M.S. in Communication Disorders, and a Ph.D. in Psychological Sciences from The University of Texas at Dallas. Dr. Shepard's research focuses on infant social-communicative development with an emphasis on the mother-infant relationship in face and language processing. Dr. Shepard has worked with infants and children who have a variety of developmental delays and disorders in early childhood intervention, public and private schools, and home health.

Tina L. Stanton-Chapman, Ph.D., is a Professor and Associate Director of the Early Childhood Education and Human Development program at the University of Cincinnati. She is also on the Fulbright Specialist roster for the U.S. Department of Defense. Her research centers on improving the peer relationships of children with disabilities on playground settings. This work includes the development of new playground equipment that meets the needs of children of all abilities.

Colby D. Taylor is an Assistant Professor of Behavioral Sciences at Christian Brothers University and a Pediatric Fellow at the University of Tennessee Health Sciences Center's Boling Center for Developmental Disabilities. He received his doctorate in School Psychology from the University of Memphis in 2015. His research interests focus on oral reading fluency and on developmental aspects of Autism Spectrum Disorder.

Mark Terjesen is an Associate Professor at St. John's University in the School Psychology (PsyD and MS) programs. Dr. Terjesen has studied, published, and presented at a number of national and international conferences and trained many professionals internationally in school psychology, ADHD, and the use of cognitive behavioral practices with children and families. Dr. Terjesen has served as President of the School Division of the New York State Psychological Association, the President of the Trainers of School Psychologists, and is Past President of Division 52 (International Psychology) of the American Psychological Association of which he is also a fellow.

Jun Wang is an Assistant Professor in the Department of Recreation, Park, and Tourism Sciences at Texas A&M University. Her research focuses on the positive development of children and adolescents from diverse socio-cultural backgrounds and the impact of socialization processes, such as parent-child interactions and out-of-school time activities.

Hannah Wurster, Ph.D., MFTC, is an infant mental health postdoctoral fellow at the One Health Institute at Colorado State University and the program manager for the Mil Dias de Amor infant mental health program at La Cocina, a nonprofit agency that delivers free-of-charge mental health services to Latinx families and families of young children. She has a doctorate in Applied Developmental Science and a master's degree in Marriage and Family Therapy, both from Colorado State University. She is a candidate for state licensure as a Marriage and Family Therapist and is endorsed by the Colorado Association for Infant Mental Health as an Infant Family Associate.

Perspectives on Early Childhood Psychology and Education

PECPE publishes twice a year, in the fall and spring. These two issues on specific focuses are typically guest-edited and can also include a few general articles.

Editorial Policy and Submission Guidelines

Perspectives on Early Childhood Psychology and Education focuses on publishing original contributions from a broad range of psychological and educational perspectives relevant to infants, young children (to age 8 years), families, and caregivers. Manuscripts incorporating evidence-based research, theory, and practice within clinical, community, developmental, neurological, and school psychology perspectives are considered. In addition, the journal accepts test and book reviews, literature reviews, program descriptions and evaluations, clinical studies, and other professional materials of interest to psychologists and educators working with young children. Proposals for special focus topics may be made to the Editor.

Format: Manuscripts should be original work not currently submitted for publication to other journals. Authors must follow the guidelines of the *Publication Manual of the American Psychological Association* (Sixth Edition). Manuscripts may not exceed 35 double-spaced pages in length, including the cover page, abstract, references, tables, and figures.

Submission: Submit an electronic copy of the manuscript for editorial review. Avoid including any identifying author information in the text. Selection of manuscripts is based on blind peer review. Include a cover page with the following information: the title of article, author(s) full name(s), title(s), institution or professional affiliations, and mailing and email address of primary author. The cover page will not be sent to reviewers.

Selection Criteria:

- Importance of topic in early childhood psychology and education
- Theory and research related to content
- Contribution to professional practice in early childhood psychology and education
- Clear and concise writing

Submit manuscripts to the Editor electronically at the following email address: PECPE@bsu.edu.

CALL FOR PAPERS

We are seeking a special focus for the Spring 2020 issue of *PECPE*. If you are interested in submitting a topic and being the guest editor, please send a brief (approximately 250 words) proposal to me, Dr. David E. McIntosh, Editor, *PECPE* (PECPE@bsu.edu) for consideration.

Special focus and general manuscripts for the Fall 2019 issue are due **August 15, 2019**. Manuscripts should be original work not currently submitted for publication to other journals. Authors must follow the guidelines of the *Publication Manual of the American Psychological Association* (Sixth Edition). Manuscripts may not exceed 35 double-spaced pages in length, including the cover page, abstract, references, tables, and figures. Avoid including any identifying author information in the text. Selection of manuscripts is based on blind peer review. Include a cover page with the following information: the title of article, author(s) full name(s), title(s), institution or professional affiliations, and mailing and email address of primary author. The cover page will not be sent to reviewers.

Please share this information with your colleagues and students.

Volume 4, Issue 1 of
Perspectives on Early Childhood Psychology and Education
was published in Spring 2019
by Pace University Press

Cover and Interior Design by Sara Yager
Cover and Interior Layout by Jessica Estrella
The journal was typeset in Minion and Myriad
and printed by Lightning Source

Pace University Press
Director: Manuela Soares
Associate Director: Stephanie Hsu
Marketing Manager: Patricia Hinds
Design Consultant: Sara Yager

Graduate Assistants: Jessica Estrella and Alicia Hughes
Graduate Student Aide: Daren Fleming

www.ingramcontent.com/pod-product-compliance
Lightning Source LLC
Chambersburg PA
CBHW061451300426
44114CB00014B/1934